"An excellent book for anyone who wants to bring more consciousness into the way they work and improve their effectiveness and the way others respond to them."

—*Giles Bateman, former chairman of CompUsa and cofounder of Price Club*

"*Watercooler Wisdom* is an inspiring book that is both well researched and thoughtful. It provides excellent principles and practices that will engage you and show you how to transform the experience of stress in the workplace into personal satisfaction and prosperity. It's an essential companion for true success."

—*Lynne Twist, author of* The Soul Of Money

"This book provides a clever mirror to examine our internal thoughts and habits at work. It gives an opportunity for self-examination and advice that will be long valued by anyone who reads it."

—*Melba Pattillo Beals, author of* Warriors Don't Cry, *and winner of the Congressional Gold Medal*

"*Watercooler Wisdom* shows us in a clear and simple way that we all have the ability to have a work life that runs like a fine Swiss watch."

—*Terry Jones, founder of Travelocity*

"*Watercooler Wisdom* is an important read for anyone trying to get ahead in business or life. An insightful look at the best of human emotion at work."

—*Tom Latour, president of the Kimpton Hotel Group*

"This book gives important insight on how to thrive in today's rapidly changing business world and is a must read for aspiring young professionals or anyone wanting to have a successful career."

—*Stephen Seligman, chief executive officer of*
The Learning Annex

"This book provides the kind of guidance that when taken to heart helps both seasoned workers and young people entering the work force develop excellent work habits for a lifetime of success and satisfaction."

—*Maddy Dychtwald, cofounder of Age Wave*
and author of Cycles: How We Will Live,
Work, and Buy

"Smart people will *love* this book. Like a series of brilliant coaching sessions, each tailored exactly to your personal needs, *Watercooler Wisdom* will put you on the positive side of change."

—*Raz Ingrasci, president and CEO of The*
Foundation

"Bailey and Leland are talented communicators who blend insightful stories gathered from real-life experience with practical, immensely helpful advice. This book is a how-to for solving the everyday workplace issues that plague most of us. It is an enjoyable read cover to cover or picked up and used as a resource guide."

—*Michelle Blieberg, global learning officer with*
UBS Investment Bank

"*Watercooler Wisdom* is one of the most practical, useful applications of spiritual principles for business and the workplace."

—*Brenda Wade, author of* Power Traces

watercooler
WISDOM

how

smart people

prosper in the face

of conflict, pressure

& change

KEITH BAILEY & KAREN LELAND

New Harbinger Publications, Inc.

Publisher's Note

This publication is designed to provide accurate and authoritative information in regard to the subject matter covered. It is sold with the understanding that the publisher is not engaged in rendering psychological, financial, legal, or other professional services. If expert assistance or counseling is needed, the services of a competent professional should be sought.

Distributed in Canada by Raincoast Books.

Copyright © 2006 by Keith Bailey and Karen Leland
New Harbinger Publications, Inc.
5674 Shattuck Avenue
Oakland, CA 94609
www.newharbinger.com

Cover design by Amy Shoup
Cover image by Todd Pearson/Photodisc Red/Getty Images
Text design by Amy Shoup and Michele Waters-Kermes
Acquired by Catharine Sutker
Edited by Amy Johnson

Printed in the United States of America

Library of Congress Cataloging-in-Publication Data

Bailey, Keith, 1945-
  Watercooler wisdom : how smart people prosper in the face of conflict, pressure, and change / Keith Bailey and Karen Leland.
      p. cm.
  Includes bibliographical references and index.
  ISBN 1-57224-436-4
  1. Job stress. 2. Work—Psychological aspects. 3. Quality of work life. 4. Work environment. I. Leland, Karen. II. Title.
  HF5548.85.B355 2005
    158.7—dc22
                              2005031183

07 06 05

10 9 8 7 6 5 4 3 2 1

First printing

To my brother Mel. Thank you for being there when I couldn't.

—Keith

To my husband Jon, for loving me through all of it. And to my girlfriend Liza—thanks for all those brainstorming breakfasts at Comforts.

—Karen

CONTENTS

PART 3
CONFLICT: SMART PEOPLE DANCE WITH FIRE

PART 4

THE MINI-MAKEOVERS

ACKNOWLEDGMENTS

Our deepest debt of gratitude goes to the clients we have worked with over the past twenty years. From the small business owners and entrepreneurs to the corporate executives, they have inspired us with their courage and determination to make a difference in environments that often honor the traditional far more than the forward-thinking.

Many thanks to our senior associate and lead trainer, Kaylyn Lehmann, whose keen observations and commitment to skillful communication have contributed greatly to Sterling Consulting Group, us personally, and this book.

And thanks, too, to the many people who contributed their wisdom, knowledge, and support to this book, including: James Flaherty, Ty and Sarah Powers, Hal and Gigi Kaufman, Dr. Alyse Danis, Dr. Frances Vaughan, Dr. Charles D. Spielberger, Liza Ingrasci, Randy Martin, Catharine Sutker, and the team at New Harbinger.

Lastly, no acknowledgment would be complete without a heartfelt thank you to our spouses, Deborah and Jon. They watched, worried, and supported us throughout the ups and downs of creation and execution. Now that we have come up for air, their strength and commitment to our success are appreciated beyond words.

INTRODUCTION

For most of us, life at work is very busy—that's why it's called our place of bus-i-ness! From the moment we walk into the office we are consumed; our day is filled with deadlines, meetings, pressures, and politics—and these days a lot of uncertainty, too. So it's hardly surprising that in the middle of this whirlwind of activity we forget how powerful we really are—we forget the natural ability and power each of us has to transform our experience of our workday from frustrating to fulfilling, regardless of the distractions and circumstances around us. *Watercooler Wisdom: How Smart People Prosper in the Face of Conflict, Pressure, and Change* is about reclaiming that power.

Writing a book to help people deal with work stress has been a recurring idea for both of us for many years. Yet—not having a book such as this to guide us!—we never found ourselves able to break free from the endless busyness and actually *do* anything about it. Then, one fateful day, we decided to go on a residential meditation retreat. At the end of the retreat, after not talking to anyone for a week, Karen smiled and said, "I know the title of our book. It came to me as I was meditating: *Watercooler Wisdom.*"

The title somehow brought the book alive in a new way. We began the preliminary work of gathering data from the vast and various company surveys we had conducted over the years. The result of this work we call the Sterling Study.

THE STERLING STUDY: 20,000 PEOPLE CAN'T BE WRONG

Over the past twenty years, as the founders of Sterling Consulting Group, we've had the opportunity to meet and speak with tens of thousands of people—in our training programs, speeches, and consulting work. In particular, we've had the privilege of surveying approximately 20,000 executives, managers, staff, and customers in one-on-one interviews, focus groups, telephone interviews, written questionnaires, and, more recently, Web-based surveys. The companies for whom we have conducted these surveys range from small businesses to some of the largest corporations in the world. They are from a wide variety of industries including: health care, banking, government, high-tech, transportation, insurance, financial services, travel, pharmaceutical, manufacturing, retail, and many others. We have conducted these surveys all over the world, in the United States, the United Kingdom, Southeast Asia, Western Europe, Eastern Europe, the Middle East, Latin America, and Africa. Surveys focused on a variety of core business issues, including: employee satisfaction, customer satisfaction, management effectiveness, and change management.

What we have learned from interviewing these many, many people has profoundly changed the coaching and consulting we provide to our clients, the way we run our business, and our personal work practices. While we did not set out to specifically study conflict, pressure, and change at work, these areas developed into such significant trends that this book is the result. It's not our aim in this book to provide statistical information from the study, but rather, anecdotal information. There are plenty of surveys out there that quote useful and interesting statistics relating to overall work issues—in fact, we have cited many of them in this book. Our intention in gathering all of this information and putting it in *Watercooler Wisdom* is to present to the reader what we have learned about how smart people prosper in the face of conflict, pressure, and change. (For the purposes of this book, our definition of prosperity is the bigger picture of "a successful, flourishing, or thriving condition," not the more narrow definition of "financial success.")

The book you now have in your hands has morphed into something better, we hope, than we ever dreamed of at that retreat. Having worked in business for many years we are both keenly aware of the need most people have for a solid structure that supports the implementation of wisdom into their lives. To this end we have included practical, how-to steps that have been tried and tested by our clients over the years.

WHO ARE THESE SMART PEOPLE?

The information we have compiled in this book presents a broad range of skills that *anyone* can learn and use to prosper in the face of conflict, pressure, and change at work. Assigning these qualities to a group of super-elite smart people was simply an expedient way of presenting the material in a format that emphasized real-world solutions learned from real-world people.

On many days, as we stared at our writing and tugged at the chains that kept us anchored to our desks, we wanted to find a smart person and hurt him or her. Smart people seem to know so much—and never fall victim to the pitfalls of everyday work life! Alas, there was nobody to knock off their pedestal: there isn't one particular smart person that embodies *all* of the qualities, principles, and practices in this book. There are, however, many people we have met, worked with, and interviewed who have mastered *specific* skills for dealing with conflict, pressure, and change—and prospering in the face of them.

Throughout the book we have used individual examples and case studies to help clarify and deepen the skills and principles we are presenting. Because we have all read essentially useful books that have been spoiled by sagas that resemble soap operas more than case studies, we've tended toward brevity; in some cases this meant creating composites of various people and events. As is the case with most books of this nature, names have been changed to protect the privacy of those individuals who were kind enough to share their stories with us.

HOW TO USE THIS BOOK

It's important to recognize that all of the principles and practices outlined in this book have a relationship with one another. Each one of them builds upon, strengthens, and supports the others. While you may currently excel in one area (say, dealing with pressure) you may be less than stellar in another (e.g. handling conflict). By considering all of the information in this book you will both learn new skills and enhance abilities you already possess. Having said that, there are three basic ways of using this book.

The first way is the traditional way: start at the beginning and continue through until you have reached the end. This will give you a solid understanding of the material contained within the book and each set of skills you learn will automatically build on the ones presented before them. Afterwards, you may find it beneficial to revisit those parts that are particularly relevant to your current work situation.

The second way is to complete the Prosperity at Work Index (found in Start Smart) and then focus on reading those parts of the book that address the areas you've identified as needing some work. Afterwards, you can read the remaining chapters for support of the material you have already learned.

The third way is to simply go straight to the part that will help you address a current problem at work with conflict, pressure, or change .

Lastly, we want you to remember that prospering in the face of conflict, pressure, and change doesn't mean walking around wearing an artificial smile of denial. To prosper, in our book, means to do well and grow—even when prevailing circumstances seem to conspire to your downfall. Ultimately, when we look inward to ourselves for solutions rather than endlessly waiting for the circumstances to change, we all become smarter people.

It is our sincere hope that the principles, practices, case studies, and examples presented here will inspire and empower you to have a more prosperous, productive, and satisfying work life.

Karen Leland and Keith Bailey

START SMART

THE ANATOMY OF STRESS AT WORK: CONFLICT, PRESSURE, AND CHANGE

In 1992, a United Nations report called job stress "the 20th century epidemic" ; six years later, in 1998, the World Health Organization declared job stress a "world wide epidemic" .

We've been working with companies large and small for over twenty years now, and during that time we've seen stress levels increase dramatically. We've spoken with staff members who live with a quiet but constant anxiety about job security and what unwanted changes the future may hold. We've listened to employees already so overwhelmed with work they barely have time to take a breath talk about budget cuts, increased responsibilities, and a slow erosion of job satisfaction. We've watched as well-intentioned colleagues succumb to the urgency of producing quick results—and end up in conflict instead of collaboration.

According to a survey by the Families and Work Institute (2005), one in three Americans is chronically overworked; 54 percent of workers have felt overwhelmed at some point in the past month by how much work they have to do. "In some sense things are getting worse," says Ellen Galinsky, president of the Families and Work Institute: "People are working longer hours and their jobs are becoming more demanding." And the cost isn't just personal: the American Institute of Stress (1999) estimates that stress annually costs U.S. businesses $300 billion in accidents, absenteeism, employee turnover, insurance, legal fees, and lost productivity.

The bad news is it doesn't look as if the everyday stress of our work environments is going to lessen anytime soon—and hoping that better circumstances will provide stress relief is like hoping we will go back to the horse and buggy as a solution to ending air pollution! Instead, we need to develop the skills and knowledge to thrive in our frenzied work environments.

Stress Isn't One Thing, It's Three

According to the National Mental Health Association

Much of our stress comes from less dramatic everyday responsibilities. Obligations and pressures that are both physical and mental are not always obvious to us. In response to these daily strains your body automatically increases blood pressure, heart rate, respiration, metabolism, and blood flow to your muscles. This response is intended to help your body react quickly and effectively to a high-pressure situation. However, when you are constantly reacting to stressful situations without making adjustments to counter the effects, you will feel stress that can threaten your health and well-being. Stress can cause physical, emotional, and behavioral disorders which can affect your health, vitality, peace-of-mind, as well as personal and professional relationships. Too much stress can cause relatively minor illnesses like insomnia, backaches, or headaches, and can contribute to potentially life-threatening diseases like high blood pressure and heart disease.

CONFLICT PRESSURE CHANGE

Although *work stress* is a generally accepted term that covers a broad range of physical, emotional, and psychological experiences, based on our findings in the Sterling Study (discussed in the introduction) we have defined *workplace stress* in a more specific and targeted way: in our experience, what most people mean when they talk about workplace stress is three things: conflict, pressure, and change, occurring either individually or all at once. Since the one thing that's constant is change, let's start with that.

Change

Change comes in all shapes and sizes. Even comparatively mundane changes—a new computer system, a change of meeting time, a new desk location, working on a day off, or a cancelled appointment—can send some people into a tailspin. For others, it may take a bigger change—being moved into a new department, getting a new boss, relocating, being taken over by another company, or being laid off—to start the stress machinery moving.

Barbara, VP of Human Resources for a large financial institution: *We were a company of seven hundred people that was acquired by a company that has eleven thousand employees. I see a lot of people getting frustrated by new, less flexible processes; for instance,* *we used to be able to hire a new employee in four days, now it takes three weeks. A lot of my job is helping people through the fear, anger, and anxiety that these changes can bring.*

Chester, an airport security supervisor: *Almost every day I'm having to implement new procedures—and that becomes stressful for me and my staff. They are less able to focus on their jobs with all the constant change.*

Bryana, a graphic designer: *In my business, clients expect me to be up on the latest design technology. I have to update my software frequently in order to stay current. I enjoy learning new things, but I find with all the technology changes I have less confidence in my skills than I used to.*

In our research, the single most significant quality we found in smart people who successfully manage change at work is the ability to be a *central player*. Central players are willing to be bigger than their circumstances by refusing to blame outside forces for their predicament. Central players look within at what they are feeling and discover innovative and empowering ways to resolve the challenges that changes bring.

In part 1, we'll look closely at what it means to be a central player and explore various other critical skills smart people utilize to respond to change with intelligence and integrity.

Pressure

Typically, businesspeople we meet at conferences, clients we consult with, and the managers and staff we interview all describe pressure at work as having too much to do, in too little time, with too little resources. They are so busy that they no longer feel a sense of satisfaction or accomplishment. Most experience an imbalance between meeting their work goals and having time to pursue personal goals; many know what they have to do but just can't seem to get it done.

Charlene, a lawyer with a national law firm: *Sometimes I can have upwards of forty clients at one time and my days disappear in a flurry of activity. I answer my emails at home in the evening—I even took my Blackberry with me on our family vacation! I'm finding that my personal life is beginning to suffer. I have to do something to relieve the pressure and make it possible to spend more quality time with my family.*

Bill, a veterinary assistant: *Ours is a small but busy office. I spend every day dealing with pet owners, scheduling emergency visits, and dealing with a million interruptions. I love what I do but I get frustrated at not having any time to do the projects that are important but less urgent—projects that would make this office even more efficient.*

Wendy, a training specialist with a semiconductor company: *We've had several cutbacks in the past two years. My department used to have eight people, now I'm the only one left. Every day is a challenge. I've asked for help but there isn't a budget for more head count in this area. I don't know what to do. I've been with this company for seven years and I don't want to quit but the pressure is really getting to me.*

Not surprisingly, we've found these kinds of work pressures prevalent at all levels and in every industry—even in every country! Although many of the people we spoke to seemed to constantly teeter at the edge of chaotic collapse, there were others—sometimes even in the same department—who seemed better able to handle the pressures of their workload and operate with a higher degree of efficiency, effectiveness, and overall job satisfaction. In part 2, we'll focus on how you can manage your energy, goals, and values to bring more sanity and order to an overwhelming workplace—and, as a result, to your life.

Conflict

Conflict at its most innocuous presents itself in the workplace either as an unwillingness to speak up or as a simple difference of personality, opinion, or style. However, these innocent beginnings more often than not bring about misunderstandings that then escalate into anger and intolerance. By learning how to manage our relationships with others—especially those we find difficult or unaccommodating—we can minimize conflict and increase our capacity for open-mindedness.

Sue, a call center supervisor: *I find that a big part of my job is talking to my agents after they've spoken to a particularly angry customer. These types of conversations usually leave them stressed and upset. I advise them not to take it personally but to get better at learning how to steer the conversation away from confrontation.*

Phil, a customer service representative for an insurance company: *I am pretty good at dealing with most people but there are certain customers where as soon as I hear their voice, I just feel myself tense up. The minute they start speaking I have a really strong impulse to say something rude and hang up the phone! Of course, I resist the urge and try to be professional but my* *attitude must have a negative affect on the conversation. It definitely has an effect on my mood at work.*

Greta, an administrative assistant: *One of the managers I work with is always teasing me about how quiet I am. I want to tell her to be quiet and leave me alone but I'm afraid that I'd end up making her mad. This causes me enormous amounts of worry and strain at work. I wish I knew a good way to approach her about this!*

Philosopher and psychologist William James once said, "Whenever you're in conflict with someone, there is one factor that can make the difference between damaging your relationship and deepening it. That factor is attitude." In part 3, we'll present techniques and practices that will help you maintain an attitude that fosters rapport and understanding in a wide range of conflict situations. Conflict at work is inevitable, but alienating coworkers, upsetting customers, and elevating your stress level is not!

THE PROSPERITY AT WORK INDEX

The journey of making your work life more enjoyable, satisfying, and productive begins with taking an honest inventory of what is working both for and against your prosperity at work! (As we discussed in the introduction, we're talking about prosperity in the big-picture sense of "a successful, flourishing, or thriving condition," and not the more common definition of "financial success.")

Over the past twenty years, we've had the opportunity to speak with thousands of people from different countries, different industries, and different levels about the quality of their work lives. Consistently, these interviews, focus groups, and surveys have revealed that those who prosper in the face of conflict, pressure, and change—smart people—possess three essential abilities.

We believe that these three abilities are at the heart of satisfaction and success at work.

The twenty-one statements in the Prosperity at Work Index represent the leading indicators for each of the three essential abilities that relate to conflict, pressure, and change. By taking the questionnaire and creating your personal profile, you will be empowered to use the principles, practices, and techniques provided in this book with greater focus.

Are you ready to get started? Consider the following statements and rate your level of agreement with each statement on a scale of 1 to 7. As you go through the statements keep the following in mind:

- Score these statements in the context of your work life and business relationships rather than marriage and friendships.

- To get an accurate score, please rate *all* the statements. If a certain statement does not seem to apply to you at the present, think of a time when it did and answer based on that previous relevant experience.

- In cases where the statements have multiple parts, base your rating on the *whole* statement.

- As much as possible, consider your current circumstances at work, not how it has been in the past (or how you hope it will be in the future!).

- Only use whole numbers to score; don't use fractions.

- Remember: the more honest your responses, the more accurate your score.

1	2	3	4	5	6	7
Never			Sometimes			Always

_____ **A.** I believe that I have the power to affect the quality of my life at work and that my attitude and actions make a difference in my satisfaction, enjoyment, and productivity on the job.

_____ **B.** When I am working on a big project, I experience satisfaction and a sense of accomplishment throughout the process, not just at the end.

_____ **C.** If I have a negative opinion of someone I can usually put it aside in order to work with them to get the job done.

_____ **A.** When I am faced with an upsetting or unexpected event at work, after an initial emotional response I usually see it as an opportunity for growth and rebound quickly.

_____ **B.** Regardless of the inevitable ups and downs, I leave work at the end of most days with a sense of accomplishment and achievement.

_____ **C.** When I experience anger I tend not to dwell on it, but instead let go of it fairly quickly, moving on and redirecting my energy.

_____ **A.** When things go wrong at work, rather than blame others I try to look at the whole picture—including what I may have done or not done to contribute to the situation.

_____ **B.** I regularly set personal and professional goals and I am in the habit of taking daily and/or weekly actions to achieve them.

_____ **C.** I am comfortable and flexible enough with my own style to get along and work with a diverse group of people who have varying personalities and styles.

_____ **A.** Even when busy, I make a habit of taking the time to reflect on my objectives and the best course of action before taking steps to resolve a problem.

_____ **B.** When prioritizing my daily to-do items, I make sure that I assign a high priority to at least one or two items that will help me achieve my goals, but are not necessarily urgent.

_____ **C.** When something upsets me, rather than just reacting on the spot, I will take time away to determine how best to handle the situation.

_____ **A.** Even though I may be afraid of failing, my fear doesn't stop me from taking on big, new, or exciting challenges that will help me grow.

_____ **B**. Regardless of the degree of acknowledgment I may receive, I believe that the work I do and/or the way in which I do it makes a contribution.

_____ **C.** When my opinion differs from that of another person, I am able to assert my own ideas as well as consider and respect the ideas of others—without discounting views that are simply different than my own.

_____ **A.** When I find myself thinking about something over and over, I make a point to look beyond my thoughts to the feelings that are involved.

_____ **B.** I feel energized and organized when I walk into my personal work area (desk, cubical, office).

_____ **C.** If I am upset with someone—or about something—I make it a point to communicate with them directly and resolve it.

_____ **A.** When I am faced with a challenge I make it a point to seek out mentors, coaches, and others who will support me in learning, growing, and succeeding.

_____ **B.** I am aware of those times of the day when my energy level is naturally higher or lower, and plan activities that require a high level of focus accordingly.

_____ **C.** When someone is angry with me I am able to listen to what they have to say—even if I may disagree or be upset by it.

Scoring the Index

Now that you have finished scoring each statement individually, total the scores for the A, B, and C statements separately.

My total A score is: _____

My total B score is: _____

My total C score is: _____

Each one of your three separate scores (A, B, and C) represents a specific ability. Read the descriptions below to see where you stand.

Change: Smart People Are Central Players (A Statements)
Score _____

The changes you experience at work (both big and small) can dramatically affect your point of view, mood, and energy level. New circumstances bring new challenges, yet no matter how joyous or upsetting they may be, you have an option about how you choose to think about and respond to the changes you face. Smart people know that dealing with external change is an internal game that requires clarity of feelings, the ability to reflect, and self-determination. They also know that making an internal change requires a motivation greater than just wanting to make it happen and an ability to keep going when the going gets rough.

The A statements focus on your self-determination, inner strength, and how well you manage yourself on the job, including how you deal with the turbulent terrain of change.

Pressure: Smart People Create Tomorrow Today (B Statements)
Score _____

Creating goals (both personal and professional), setting priorities, and developing habits of action empower you to manage the pressures of your workload and help make today's aspirations tomorrow's reality. Have you noticed, however, that it's hard to create something new, different, and exciting in the future when your focus and energy today are so diluted? By tying up loose ends and removing the distracting tangles they create, you free up your energy.

The B statements focus on how good a job you are doing at keeping the pressures of work at bay by cleaning up the clutter—mentally and physically—and the degree to which you purposefully use your time and energy to create and pursue your goals.

Conflict: Smart People Dance with Fire (C Statements)
Score _____

Knowing how to communicate and develop relationships with

others is an essential skill that helps you make things happen. It's tempting to think that your work life would be a lot easier if it wasn't for all those other people—colleagues, bosses, customers—who are so demanding, unreasonable, and frustrating (if only they'd leave you alone to get your job done!). Smart people know that to prosper at work they must be skilled at reaching out and connecting even with those they have conflict with.

Many people deal with conflict by not dealing with it. While this strategy may keep you all cozy in your comfort zone, it doesn't do much for moving you into the satisfaction zone. Dealing with conflict is not a mystery; it's a dance with specific steps that help create harmony and understanding—if you know how to read and respond to your partner's tempo. Smart people practice these steps and have the confidence to speak up, be heard, keep listening, and stay engaged, no matter how heated the circumstances.

The C statements focus on how well you create rapport with others and handle the hot topics of conflict, anger, and disagreement in the workplace.

Create Your Personal Profile

The personal profile is a pie chart that reflects your overall prosperity at work. Take the three scores above and plot each one in its relevant section. The circles are numbered to make it easier for you to mark where your score would approximately fall. Draw a line across the section that intersects with your scoring mark. You might want to shade each part of the pie for clarity and comparison (see example).

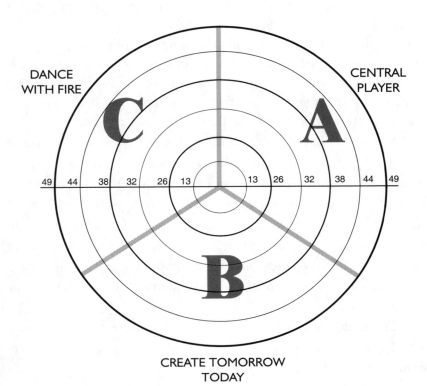

DANCE
WITH FIRE

CENTRAL
PLAYER

C

A

49 44 38 32 26 13 13 26 32 38 44 49

B

CREATE TOMORROW
TODAY

Example

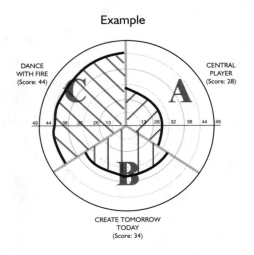

DANCE
WITH FIRE
(Score: 44)

CENTRAL
PLAYER
(Score: 28)

C

A

49 44 38 32 26 13 13 26 32 38 44 49

B

CREATE TOMORROW
TODAY
(Score: 34)

Once you have your three scores recorded on the chart, you may find that they are fairly equal, or that some may be more or less than others. The closer the shading is to the outer edge of the circle, the stronger the ability. On the other hand, if you have an area where the shading is closer to the center of the circle, that ability is weaker. Here's what the scores mean:

39–49 Points. Scoring in this zone means you are aware of and actively using these abilities. You might find it useful to get a second opinion by having a coworker score the statements. Staying in this zone is an ongoing process, and there are always new principles to be learned and new skills to be gained. We suggest you use the information in this book to build on the strong foundation you already have.

27–38 points. Scoring in this zone indicates that you are aware of this ability but not using it to its full advantage. In this zone, a little effort goes a long way. You are in the perfect position to leverage the progress you have already made in this area. Use the information in this book to focus on improving one or two specific skills that would increase your prosperity at work.

0–26 points. A score in this zone is a heads up that you are unaware of and/or underutilizing this ability at work. Take some time to reflect on this ability and how increasing it would impact your life. You may also want to talk with a close friend or colleague about ways you could improve. Use the information in this book to bring new awareness to this ability and to create a plan for actively improving your skills in this area.

PART I

CHANGE: SMART PEOPLE ARE CENTRAL PLAYERS

What lies behind us and what lies before us are small matters when compared to what lies within us.

—Ralph Waldo Emerson

CHAPTER 1

FACING THE CHALLENGE: FROM PREDICAMENT TO PROSPERITY

In *Leadership and the New Science*, Meg Wheatley declares:

> ... disorder can be a source of order ... growth is found in disequilibrium, not in balance. The things we fear most in organizations—fluctuations, disturbances, imbalances—need not be signs of an impending disorder that will destroy us. Instead, fluctuations are the primary source of creativity. (1994)

With hindsight it's easy to see that disequilibrium can lead to growth. However, in the heat of the moment, when faced with conflict, pressure, or change at work, the challenge is to stay present and focused on prospering. Smart people have developed a high tolerance for this disequilibrium along with a willingness to leave their comfort zone. They realize that the challenge to prosper and grow—even when it's scary or unexpected—is an opportunity to be more satisfied and successful in the long run. Rather than run from these situations they have sharpened their understanding of how to recognize and navigate the bumpy emotional road from predicament to prosperity.

UNEXPECTED AND DISRUPTIVE EVENTS

These are those events and situations in the course of work that are initiated by others that impact your work life. For example, you may learn that your office is being relocated from the West Coast to the East Coast, or that the seven-month timeline you were given to design a new inventory system has now been shortened to four months by your new boss.

When you experience unexpected and disruptive events, having a road map to guide you through the roller-coaster ride of common challenges and emotions is essential.

Stage 1: Initial Impact

When we are first confronted with a situation that is not of our own making but negatively impacts us, our first reaction is often confusion or bewilderment—a feeling of being smacked on the side of the head! Imagine, for example, that you've had a really productive day and are feeling great. Your boss catches you before you leave and asks to have a few words. He or she carefully explains that your company is being bought by another organization and there is going to be a workforce reduction of 50 percent! Your boss goes on to explain that it's too early to know who will go and who will stay

---

INITIAL IMPACT CHEAT SHEET

- Accept that confusion, bewilderment, and disorientation are a natural part of this phase.
- Don't make any rash decisions.
- Don't take on any high profile actions.
- Talk with a friend/loved one about what happened and how you feel about it.
- If there's nobody to talk to then write down your thoughts.

but you can be certain some big changes are about to happen.

As the news hits, you experience a flood of feelings and thoughts. Your head is spinning. What you thought you knew collides with this new reality. The carpet has been pulled from under you. You grope for understanding. Your adrenaline surges and you feel confused—for minutes, hours, days, or even weeks.

CASE STUDY: Ken and the Restaurant

Ken was an assistant manager at a large theme restaurant. The owner, Alan, was a demanding and rigorous taskmaster who seemed to appreciate Ken's laid-back style, but nevertheless expected him to manage the staff of seventy-five with an iron fist. Ken worked with two other assistant managers, both of whom, in Ken's young (and somewhat arrogant) opinion, did not have the communication skills or the staff loyalty that he enjoyed.

At one Tuesday management meeting Alan announced to the three assistant managers that he was going to be spending less time at the restaurant and would be promoting one of them to a full manager position. Ken was sure it would be him. And when he was asked to join his boss for lunch at a fancy yacht club restaurant, he figured the deal was as good as done.

Wearing his best suit, he arrived at lunch and listened as Alan spoke about his plans for the restaurant, his dreams about creating a cohesive management team, and so on. Ken was waiting for the promotional punch line. Well, the punch line delivered quite a punch: Alan then methodically and reasonably explained that Ken's style didn't really work for what he had in mind, that because Ken was not a team player, he was letting him go—at once. He apologized and said that he would pay Ken two full months' salary, but he would like Ken to pick up his things from the restaurant immediately after lunch. That was it: Ken was fired!

Ken's confusion was total. As if in a dream, he collected his belongings and went home. His world was so rocked he had difficulty focusing on the drive home. Ken called his wife and explained what had happened. Outwardly he ranted and raved; inwardly he wept with despair.

Give Yourself Time

When faced with a sudden and shocking predicament, it's not a good idea to make any rash decisions, take any high profile actions, or say anything that you might later—when you're more sane—regret. Being smart at this initial stage means allowing yourself the time to go through the natural feelings of confusion and disorientation.

Since your brain will be working a mile a minute, ruminating over all the possible outcomes and problems that the situation has spawned, the act of sharing your thoughts and feelings with trusted friends and loved ones is particularly important. Talking things out is helpful not because it necessarily solves the problem, but because it helps you relieve internal pressure and adjust mentally and emotionally to what is happening.

Be warned: your conversation during this stage may not make a lot of sense or be particularly lucid! Choosing a good friend or family member as your listener frees you from worrying about saying anything compromising—and gives you free rein to vent away until you gain your composure. If you don't have someone you can talk to, write down your thoughts and feelings in a journal. The secret to this type of journaling is writing down *exactly* what comes into your head. Don't edit or judge—just write.

Stage 2: Reality Hits Home

Emotionally, this is usually the most uncomfortable part of the predicament to prosperity process. As the shock subsides you are left with a stark new reality. The true consequences of the situation come to light and you may have to deal with losing the familiar and expected, whether it be a routine, a colleague, or your surroundings.

In the case study above, as the reality of Ken's sudden departure from the restaurant hit home, he had the same thoughts over and over again: How long had the other two managers been plotting his downfall? Only a fool (Alan) would fire someone as smart and talented as him.... How would he ever get another job now that he had "Fired!" branded across his resume? How would he pay the mortgage? On a deeper level he grieved the loss of working with the servers and cooks he liked, the familiarity of the daily restaurant routines, and seeing the regular customers he had come to know.

Anger and Fear

Anger and fear are among the most common emotions we feel in this reality phase. Anger may manifest itself as blame. For example, Ken was convinced that he was fired by fools. Never once

> **REALITY HITS HOME CHEAT SHEET**
> - Be aware of any feelings of anger and fear you may have.
> - Don't avoid your feelings, feel them—all of them!
> - Don't focus on long-term goals; instead, keep a daily to-do list.

did Ken look at what he had contributed to—or could learn from—the situation. Also, his underlying feelings were so strong during this time he fell into the trap of trying to avoid them. Ken was far more comfortable with his anger than with the sadness and loss he was feeling underneath. Ken was missing the single skill that would have most empowered him to negotiate through this process: the ability to acknowledge and feel his feelings. (In chapter 2: From Horizontal Thinking to Vertical Feeling, we show you how to improve this skill.)

In addition to the anger and fear we often feel in this stage, certainty and stability of the future are often missing, and long-term goals can seem overwhelming. Switching to short-term tasks can be beneficial—something as simple as keeping a daily to-do list can provide a manageable reality to hold onto. If you keep some kind of paper or electronic planner, we recommend using it frequently and diligently at this stage. Focusing on doing what you know needs to be done, no matter how trivial it may seem, can help reduce your anxiety.

Ken's post-restaurant weeks were filled with long-term fantasies—move to another country, buy the restaurant and fire his imagined adversaries, etc.—but in the end, he relied on the simple yet important daily tasks to get him through: he updated his resume, searched online job postings, made a list of networking possibilities, etc.

Stage 3: Integration

Eventually the intensity you feel in stage 2 begins to lighten up and you see flickers of light at the end of the tunnel—and they aren't the headlights of an oncoming train! As the flickers grow brighter, you'll have flashes of insight about how this predicament might actually provide you with an opportunity to prosper. It's useful to write down any pertinent insights you may have now so that you can review them later, especially when formulating future goals. Usually this period also brings with it big pendulum swings between excitement and fear: On the one hand you see whole new possibilities for your life; on the other, you have the anxiety of not really knowing how it is all going to turn out.

Seeing the Upside

As your fears and uncertainty subside, you will begin to see the upside of the situation. This will refresh your spirit and bring about a new feeling of security. This stage is an important time for developing new long-term goals. Harness your imagination and paint a mental picture of what you want to create in this new landscape that is unfolding before you!

> **INTEGRATION CHEAT SHEET**
> - Ask yourself: "What can I learn from this situation?"
> - Develop and write down long-term goals.
> - Expect big emotional pendulum swings, from fear to excitement.
> - Seek out mentors.

Now is also the perfect time to seek out mentors, coaches, and supporters who can help you grow and learn in these new opportunities you are creating. A mentor, coach, or supporter might be a friend or colleague (old or new) who is seasoned in the path you intend to travel. Often, the ideal mentor is characterized as being an older and wiser person, but we have found that great mentors, coaches, and supporters can come in all shapes and sizes as long as they have the relevant experience, compassion, and understanding.

SELF-INITIATED SIGNIFICANT EVENTS

These are the events and situations that *you* author that impact your work life. For example, you decide to change your career path to do something that holds more passion for you, or you volunteer to take on a project that you know will create pressure but ultimately cause you to grow.

Unlike predicaments that come without warning from the outside—and often with all of the subtlety of a clog-dancer—self-initiated events happen as a result of us wanting to make a shift in our work life. This type of challenge stretches us because it requires us to step beyond the familiar and increase our capacity for growth. Deciding to change careers is an example of such a challenge. While every cell in your body may be telling you to change jobs and intuitively it feels right, you have no certainty that it will turn out well. The predominant emotion is fear: fear of the unknown, fear of failing, fear of negative outcomes and consequences, and fear of losing control.

CASE STUDY: Alice and the Presentation

Alice is a recently promoted executive director of a nonprofit organization. During her many years of working in this field, she has somehow avoided having to make formal presentations to large audiences—something she fears almost more than death itself. To her horror, the days of avoidance have come to an end: She has been asked if she would be willing to make the keynote presentation to twenty-five hundred people at the annual conference. During the three months that Alice has to prepare for her thirty-minute presentation, she regularly thinks about all the things that could go wrong: she might freeze from embarrassment and forget every word that she was going to say; her presentation might not be well-received; she could be the laughing stock of the conference!

Find a Motivating Factor

Many of us, in a similar situation, might decide that the stress just wasn't worth it and withdraw from making the presentation. But when we give in to our fears we dash our chances of growing and expanding—the tremendous urge to eliminate our discomfort also diminishes our potential. But rarely is there a way of knowing for sure that everything will turn out well. No amount of preparation or planning will ever completely remove the risk factor. Smart people know that the secret to a successful stretch is finding a deeply personal motivating factor.

In this case, Alice's fearful thoughts about making the conference presentation were all focused on one outcome: whether she would fail or succeed. She was missing a core reason for making the presentation, a reason compelling enough to overshadow and weaken her fears of feeling inept before an audience. Alice's initial reason for making the conference presentation was to deliver information that she was asked to share with others in her field—a worthy sentiment but not enough to empower her to deal with the emotional stress.

Alice decided to find a "higher" purpose for making the presentation, one that was deeply personal and would help motivate her to a successful outcome. Alice began looking for a motivating factor that she believed in and that was close to her heart. After some reflection she decided that her new, overarching reason for speaking at the conference would be to inspire the audience to go back to their organizations and increase their volunteer enrollment. Volunteers were the lifeblood of the business and increasing volunteer numbers always had a positive impact on morale and efficiency. Alice became so stimulated by this opportunity to inspire that her fears—though never disappearing completely—became harmless.

Summary

► Predicaments that require us to stretch beyond the norm are natural and healthy; ultimately they provide opportunities to grow and learn.

► The key to staying grounded during times of unexpected and disruptive events is to know the stages you will go through and how to respond to them.

► When faced with an unexpected and disruptive event, we go through three main stages:

1. Initial Impact

2. Reality Hits Home

3. Integration

► The two predominant emotions associated with leaving our comfort zone are anger and fear.

► Self-initiated events are less intimidating when connected to a higher motivating factor.

CHAPTER 2

FROM HORIZONTAL THINKING TO VERTICAL FEELING

We recently learned that each of us thinks about 36,000 thoughts a day—and 98 percent of these thoughts are apparently the same thoughts that we had yesterday! This is disquieting news: how many hours, days, and weeks have we idled away in unconstructive mind-babble?

Many of these recurring thoughts involve worries and concerns about things that will probably never happen. It's easy to spend a good part of our workday negatively judging our colleagues, ourselves, and the situations we find ourselves in without even realizing it. These silent monologues (see Beware the Commentator below) can sour our good spirits and turn optimism into skepticism. And even though we may logically understand that this mind loop isn't beneficial, we keep on doing it! We have a hard time breaking the habit. This is hardly surprising, however, if you consider that most of us try to *think* our way out of thinking—which is the equivalent of complaining about people who complain: the act only compounds the condition we are trying to eliminate. The more we try and change things by "thinking positively," "thinking about something else," or "trying to forget about it," the more our mind tightens its grip and intensifies its graphic display of dismal outcomes and daunting worst-case scenarios.

Smart people know that shifting the focus of attention from their endless, unhelpful chains of thought (horizontal thinking) to the deeper level of their emotions and physical body sensations (vertical feeling) helps stop this mental merry-go-round.

BEWARE THE COMMENTATOR

One form our pervasive thoughts take is *the commentator*. The commentator is the internal narrator that silently talks to you from inside your head, the voice that has an opinion on just about everything. If you stop reading right now for a moment and stay quiet, you can listen to what your commentator's saying. It might be saying, "I don't want to stop reading, this book is too good to put down!" You get the idea.

Your commentator operates on four simple principles:

The Commentator Gets Louder When Things Aren't the Way You'd Like Them to Be

For example, if you're sitting in a theater, engrossed in a movie, and the couple in front of you start loudly discussing the plot with one another, your commentator may pop up with, "What is wrong with these people? If they don't stop I'm going to say something!" If they continue talking, you continue silently commentating: "Okay, I'm going to say something!" A few seconds later: "This is so unacceptable. I'm definitely going to say something!" And so on—until you say something, they stop, or the movie simply ends.

The Commentator Never Forgets

For example, if you lend a friend $20 and your friend then relocates to the Outer Hebrides (for reasons other than avoiding repayment!), when your friend moves back ten years later, your commentator says, "She still owes me $20!"

The Commentator Never Stops Looking for Evidence

For example, if you decide that a coworker is selfish because he or she never offers to get you a cup of coffee when they go out for theirs, then your commentator will continually and never-endingly present you with more incriminating evidence: "She *never* adds fresh paper to the fax machine." Or, "She *never* offers me a piece of her Power Bar—and she *always* eats it by my desk!"

The Commentator Accentuates the Negative

For example, if your boss gives you a dinner certificate as a thank you for doing such a stellar job, your commentator says, "It's about time the boss acknowledged me! What took him so long? I've been working for him for three years and this is the first time he's ever done anything nice!"

The commentator *does* sometimes offer us good advice, usually either by alerting us to danger or helping us look critically at things before making important decisions. But when it's just in its day-to-day idling mode, more often than not the commentator merely delivers narrow and unconstructive advice.

FIVE STEPS TO GOING VERTICAL

The following practice, broken down into five easy steps, is a powerful method for breaking a cycle of negative thinking. These simple actions can be used at work—or anywhere—to reduce anxiety, maintain a focused outlook, and free yourself from endless thoughts of the future or past so that you can rediscover that part of yourself that is alive in the present.

HORIZONTAL THOUGHTS

worry... fear ... concern ... anxiety ... doubt ... worry ... fear ... concern ... anxiety ... doubt ... worry ... fear ... concern ...

VERTICAL FEELINGS

SENSATIONS FEELINGS EMOTIONS

BODY

Step 1: Notice If Your Thoughts Are Holding You Captive

Pay attention to what you are thinking right now. Is there a recurring theme? A concern, worry, problem, regret, or judgment? Notice that you cannot stop the flow of your thoughts. Even if you really try they just keep on thinking themselves. The horrible truth is that often we aren't controlling our thoughts, our thoughts are controlling us!

Step 2: You Are More Powerful Than Your Thoughts

Imagine that all these thoughts you are observing are traveling horizontally across the front of your head like the headline ticker tape that runs along the bottom of the screen on CNN. Notice that each thought is quickly followed by the next thought, and the next, and the next, and so on. Do these thoughts provide relief, positive change, or any new or useful information? No, not usually. However, the good news is that if you are actually observing your own thought process then there must be a part of you—let's call it your inner observer—that is *not* caught up with your thought process; a part that can notice what is happening without *becoming* what's happening. Similarly, you can use this inner observer to recognize the sensations and feelings that are going on elsewhere, outside of your cranium.

Step 3: Notice Your Sensations

Move your attention vertically down from your head. Say hello to the 85 percent of yourself that exists below the neck! As soon as you move out of your horizontal thought chain, you can begin to focus on your physical sensations and inner feelings.

Start by using your inner observer to notice your breath. (If it's convenient and appropriate you can close your eyes, but it's not necessary.) Notice how you are breathing. Are your breaths shallow or deep? Long or short? Take the time to observe where you feel the strongest physical sensation of breathing—it may be in your stomach, chest, nostrils, mouth, etc. Remember that there is no correct or incorrect way of doing this, so if your mind butts in with a few wise words about how you are not doing this right, just recognize that these are horizontal thoughts—and return vertically to the sensation of breathing in your body.

After a minute or so, move your awareness to another part of your body. Notice any physical sensations. If there are lots of different sensations, focus on one at a time—maybe your stomach, your shoulders, your legs, your arms—wherever your attention is drawn. If your thoughts cut in, recognize that they are the same old headlines, nothing new, and redirect your attention to feeling the sensations in your body. Paying close attention to your breath unlocks your natural relaxing and centering abilities, and is key to going vertical.

Step 4: Feel What You Are Feeling

Now start to notice your feelings. What are the emotions you are experiencing? Maybe sadness, joy, anger, love, grief, or guilt? (Look at the Name That Feeling! section for help identifying a whole range of emotions.) Are the feelings strong or weak? Notice them without trying to fix or change anything—don't be tempted to try to snap out of it. If you notice that you feel a little sad, allow yourself to feel it: be sad. Or, if you are feeling happy, allow yourself to feel truly happy. Keep centering your focus in your body; try to be aware of your background thoughts without getting entangled in them.

Remember: a breath can always be knowingly breathed and an emotion can always be fully felt. Regardless of whether you're having a good day or a bad day at work, you *always* have the choice of where you focus your attention, and with that choice comes power.

NAME THAT FEELING!

Knowing what you are feeling is a skill that has to be learned. There are dozens and dozens of different feelings but many people cannot distinguish them clearly. When a friend asks, "How are you doing?" our response is usually "Good," "Okay," or "Fine." But by looking at the following list, you'll discover that you have many, many different feelings. Look at this list every day this week—by becoming familiar with your full range of emotions you'll improve your ability to move from horizontal thinking to vertical feeling.

Abandoned	Ambivalent	Bitter
Able	Angry	Blissful
Accomplished	Animated	Bored
Adamant	Annoyed	Brave
Adequate	Anxious	Bright
Affectionate	Apathetic	Brilliant
Afraid	Apprehensive	Bubbly
Agreeable	Awed	Burdened
Alert	Beautiful	Calm
Alone	Betrayed	Capable

Captivated	Delighted	Excited
Carefree	Desirable	Exhausted
Caring	Despair	Exhilarated
Centered	Destructive	Explosive
Challenged	Determined	Exposed
Charmed	Different	Expressive
Cheated	Diffident	Evil
Cheerful	Diminished	Fascinated
Cherished	Disagreeable	Fearful
Childish	Disappointed	Flighty
Childlike	Discontented	Flustered
Clean	Disorganized	Foolish
Clear	Distracted	Forgotten
Clever	Distraught	Frantic
Competitive	Disturbed	Free
Condemned	Dominated	Frightened
Confident	Dubious	Frustrated
Confused	Dumb	Full
Conspicuous	Eager	Fun
Contented	Ecstatic	Fury
Contrite	Electrified	Generous
Cozy	Embarrassed	Giving
Cruel	Empty	Glad
Crushed	Enchanted	Gratified
Culpable	Energetic	Greedy
Cute	Envious	Grief
Deceitful	Erotic	Grounded
Defeated	Exasperated	Guilty

Gullible	Lazy	Pressured
Happy	Lively	Pretty
Hate	Lonely	Prim
Healthy	Longing	Proud
Heavenly	Low	Quiet
Helpful	Mad	Radiant
Helpless	Mean	Rage
High	Melancholy	Real
Homesick	Miserable	Refreshed
Honored	Naughty	Rejected
Horrible	Neglected	Relaxed
Humorous	Nervous	Remorse
Hurt	Obnoxious	Responsible
Hysterical	Odd	Restless
Ignored	Open	Righteous
Impatient	Outraged	Sad
Impressed	Overwhelmed	Satisfied
Inadequate	Pain	Scared
Infuriated	Panicked	Secure
Insignificant	Patient	Selfish
Inspired	Peaceful	Serene
Integrated	Petrified	Sexy
Intimidated	Pity	Shining
Isolated	Playful	Shocked
Jealous	Pleasant	Silly
Joyous	Pleased	Skeptical
Jumpy	Powerful	Sleepy
Kind	Precarious	Sneaky

Solemn	Stupid	Terrible
Sorry	Suffering	Terrified
Spirited	Surprised	Threatened
Spiteful	Sympathetic	Thrilled
Spontaneous	Talkative	Vile
Stable	Teary	Vital
Startled	Tempted	Weak
Stingy	Tenacious	Whole
Strange	Tense	Wicked
Strong	Tentative	Yearning
Stunned	Tenuous	

Above list reprinted with permission from The Hoffman Institute.

CASE STUDY: Craig and the Monthly Bills

Every month, Craig, a small business owner, procrastinated about paying his company's bills. Just the idea of sitting at his desk and writing out checks filled him with dread. Thoughts that traveled across his brain included: "Oh —! Where's the money going to come from?" and "The months roll around so fast ..." and "These bills will never stop coming."

This procession of thoughts scrolled through Craig's brain every month, regular as clockwork—regardless of whether Craig had the money to pay the bills or not. He would try to convince himself that it would all turn out, that worrying wasn't going to help, etc. But then he would end up worrying even more! There seemed to be no escape from his monthly mental anguish until, one bill-paying day, sitting at his desk, Craig stopped what he was doing and just paid attention to his feelings and his body. "I actually sat there—pen in hand, checkbook open—and felt my fear, felt the tightness in the pit of my stomach, the hot feeling in my head, my shallow breathing. Without even trying, my negative thoughts began to weaken and fade. I wrote out my checks with a lot less of the usual mind chatter!"

Craig learned to focus on his inner feelings and physical sensations whenever he was caught up in a negative thought pattern about paying bills. As Craig says, "I've been practicing this for a while—now I can catch the negative thought patterns in a nanosecond by feeling what I'm really feeling and then moving on."

Step 5: Change Channels

Each of us experiences the world around us through four different channels: thoughts, feelings, senses, and intuition.

Thoughts

Thoughts are our intellectual and analytical channel. We use thinking to figure out problems, plan for the future, evaluate issues, etc. For example, if we are at work and we go to make copies but the copier is out of toner, we might have a thought like, "No problem, I'll reload it." Or, we might say to ourselves, "Why the heck didn't the last person deal with this?"

Feelings

Feelings are our emotional channel. Depending on the circumstances, we may feel happy, sad, peaceful, angry, etc. Using the copier scenario above, we might greet the tonerless copier with a feeling of happiness: "Yeay! I get to take time from my busy schedule and futz around with soot!" (Unlikely.) Or with anger: "I can't believe how thoughtless people can be!"

Senses

Senses are the channel that allows us to physically experience life. We use hearing, touch, taste, smell, and sight to assimilate the world around us. Back at the copier this translates into two levels of sensation: the first sensation is *seeing* the little red light that signifies an empty toner cartridge; the second sensation might be a tightening of the muscles in your neck just before your head explodes with frustration.

Intuition

Intuition is the channel most difficult to describe, and yet it plays a very important part in our lives. Webster's dictionary defines intuition as "a direct perception of truth, fact, etc., independent of any reasoning process." In the copier scenario, intuition might manifest itself as a "natural knowing" that tells you the copier isn't actually out of toner, but instead the warning light is malfunctioning.

Because work for most of us requires analysis, planning, and evaluation skills, we can easily get stuck in the thought channel—resulting in a lopsided reliance on thinking and a neglect or disregard of the other channels.

Flipping channels means deliberately choosing which area—thoughts, feelings, senses, intuition—to focus on for any given experience. We experience everything, to some degree or another, through every channel. However, because thinking is so dominant, it is useful to know that there are alternative places to focus. By moving from horizontal thinking to vertical feeling, you flip channels and allow yourself to more fully experience your-self—and in so doing, broaden the possibilities for resolution and relief.

Summary

➤ From time to time we all climb on our mental merry-go-round and replay thoughts over and over; these thoughts seem to travel horizontally across the back of our brain.

➤ Reducing the stress caused by recurring horizontal thoughts requires moving vertically down to a deeper level of physical sensations and inner feelings.

➤ There are five steps for moving from horizontal think-ing to vertical feeling:

   1. Notice if your thoughts are holding you captive

   2. Know that you are more powerful than your thoughts

   3. Notice your sensations

   4. Feel what you are feeling

   5. Change channels

➤ We have four channels through which we experience our world: thoughts, feelings, senses, and intuition; most of us focus on our thoughts to the neglect of our other channels.

CHAPTER 3

TAKING TIME TO REFLECT

At Johns Hopkins University, one of the leading universities in the United States, *reflection* is considered a critical tool. According to their Professional Development Program, "Critical reflection is an important aspect of both teaching and learning ... it is the reflection on our experiences that leads to learning—not merely the experience itself. We learn from those experiences that we ponder, explore, review, and question."

To reflect is to think carefully and seriously about something while remaining aware of the prejudices and opinions that can stop us from seeing the whole picture. When you take the time to reflect on problems, situations, and events, you learn about yourself.

Judy, a mortgage broker: *I was so relaxed and assured in the sales meeting today, I just had to take a few minutes afterwards to consider what was different and how could I recreate that state in future meetings.*

Ken, an accountant: *My coworkers often seem frustrated with me. I've spent some time thinking about this and although I hate to admit it, I'm beginning to see how some of my work habits may be contributing to their frustration.*

Laurie, a textile designer: *Today I finished a big project that involved about a dozen people in my office. As I was getting ready to go home, I started to think about how much I really enjoy and respect the people I work with.*

By reflecting, you open a window that lets you look at yourself as a central player in your own work life. You learn to look at yourself with less fear and more honesty. And this self-knowledge allows you both to overcome obstacles that would have stopped you in the past and make better choices in the future.

Unfortunately, in most of our workplaces reflection is not a skill we get much chance to practice. Rarely are we afforded the time to really think something through—even when an hour of reflection might help avoid repeating past problems, save hours of work, and reduce stress. How often are you rewarded for sitting and thinking on your job? For the most part we get praised, promoted, and paid for the results we produce and the speed at which we produce them.

In *The Fifth Discipline*, Peter Senge points out that most managers, even when they have the time, tend to devote very little energy to reflection and thus fail to learn from their mistakes. "Typically, managers adopt a strategy, then as soon as the strategy starts to run into problems, they switch to another strategy, then to another and another ... without once examining why a strategy seems to be failing" (1994).

REFLECTION IS A SKILL THAT TAKES PRACTICE

One of our clients, a manager of a large retail computer chain, took a trip to Japan to meet with his Asian counterparts. On a tour of one facility, he noticed a technician sitting at his desk staring out of the window for quite some time. Eventually our client asked his host, "How come he isn't doing anything?" "He *is* doing something," replied our client's host. "He's thinking. That's the most important part of his job."

Smart people don't believe in banging their heads against a wall—at least not once they figure out that bricks damage craniums! Instead, when faced with an important project or issue, smart people reflect on similar past situations and apply the knowledge they learn from their reflections to their current circumstances. Often, a whole new course of action is born from a few minutes spent stopping and looking. This simple practice, too often crowded out of our busy lives, gives smart people a tremendous advantage: by not repeating past mistakes, they are that much more likely to attain their objectives.

If you aren't in the practice of regular reflection but want to be, it may help you to think of it as a specific, structured activity rather than a casual series of thoughts. The first step is to decide what you want to reflect on: an abrasive conversation with a colleague, a missed deadline, an opportunity for advancement, etc. In the case study that follows, we've chosen an example where a conversation got out of hand and our reflector wants to consider both what went wrong and how she might avoid similar problems in the future.

CASE STUDY: Stephanie and the Late Coworker

Stephanie is a paralegal in a small law office. Her coworker, Janet, arrives late for work several mornings each month. As the mother of two small children, Stephanie understood how Janet's four-year-old can be a challenge to punctuality. Still, Janet is often up to an hour late.

As a result of a major case, the volume of work had almost doubled recently; Stephanie was finding herself frustrated by the added burden of coping with the department single-handedly on the mornings when Janet was late.

One particularly chaotic morning it was the last straw: Janet was late for the third time in a row and Stephanie was left trying to manage ten things at once. As soon as Janet stepped into the office, Stephanie blurted out, "It's not fair that you come into work late every day and that I have to cover the whole department on my own. I've got a crazy workload right now and I can't go on like this."

Janet was taken aback; she became defensive. "Stephanie, you get in late yourself sometimes—you know what it's like with kids. Anyway, I'm not late *every* day. And I always make up the time by staying later at the end of the day anyway."

Stephanie felt that Janet hadn't really understood the seriousness of the situation. "That's not the point! The point is that I'm being stretched every which way trying to do the work that you should be doing in the morning!"

Janet felt as if she were being backed into a corner. She retaliated, "There's plenty of things I do around here to cover *your* butt! I answer the phones and do all sorts of extra stuff after you've left for the day. I just don't moan about it!"

Stephanie and Janet both knew the conversation was going nowhere. They looked at each other for a moment and then Stephanie looked away and said, "Okay, let's talk about it later." Janet agreed, sat down at her computer, and tried to focus on her work for the day. Meanwhile, Stephanie was still cooking in her own adrenaline.

Clearly the situation wasn't resolved. Stephanie realized that she needed to have another, calmer conversation with Janet—but she was worried now that it would go downhill as fast as this first one. She decided that this was a situation that bore reflection.

Three Key Questions to Ask When Things Go Wrong—Or Right

The best way to begin a practice of reflection is to set a specific period of time (five to ten minutes is a good chunk to start with), find an environment that is quiet and free of distractions, and get comfortable.

Next, simply ask yourself a few straightforward questions. (These questions will vary somewhat depending on the situation. As you become more practiced at reflecting, you can change the questions to fit your circumstances.) In this scenario, Stephanie is reflecting about what went wrong with her conversation with Janet. However, you can also use this same process to reflect on what went *right* with a situation.

Question 1: What were your basic feelings, attitudes, and intentions in this situation?

- Were you happy, understanding, patient, upset, cynical, sad, defiant, etc.?

- Did you view the other person/people as capable, understanding, incompetent, stupid, aggressive, untrustworthy, etc.?

- Did you try to stand in others' shoes, understand diverse opinions, and be open? Or did you try to look good, prove somebody else was wrong, etc.?

- How well did you do at achieving your intentions/ objectives?

For Stephanie, the first question revealed the following: because she felt taken advantage of by Janet's lateness, she had entered the conversation with a defiant attitude. Her focus wasn't on resolving the situation, it was on proving Janet was doing something wrong.

Question 2: What, if anything, did you say that you shouldn't have? What, if anything, did you *not* say that you should have?

- Did you repeat gossip, exaggerate, blame, or condescend?

- Did you neglect an opportunity to thank, appreciate, encourage, or support?

- Was there anything else missing from the situation?

Answering this second question helped Stephanie realize that she had condescended to Janet; she'd acted like a mother scolding a child. Her comment about Janet being late "every day" was an exaggeration that would have been better off unsaid. Also, a sympathetic comment about the difficulties of being a working mother might have helped ease the tension.

Question 3: What will you do differently next time?

- How will your intention be different next time?

- What changes will you make in your attitude/behavior to be more effective?

- How would you coach another person to deal with the same situation?

With this third question, Stephanie developed some clear ideas about how to approach her next conversation with Janet. Moreover, Stephanie now committed herself to being more open to discussion.

REFLECTION EQUALS RESULTS

The following day Stephanie asked Janet if they could get together during lunch and talk. Janet agreed. At lunch there was an awkward silence until Stephanie admitted, "I hated that conversation we had yesterday. I'm sorry I was so antagonistic." Janet's face lightened. Stephanie continued, "I know that it's hard with Alex—it's just that I've always disliked multitasking so I get really stressed in the mornings when I have to do a million things."

Janet protested, "I do the same amount of hours as you. I just stay later." Stephanie heard the defensiveness in Janet's voice again—but this time she responded rather than reacted: "I know, I just want to find a solution that works for both of us. I appreciate how hard you work, and I really like working with you. There has to be an answer to this that works for both of us."

After a few long moments of silence, Janet said, "I like working with you, too. I hate to blame a four-year-old for my lateness, but he's such a handful that I have a hard time getting it together in the mornings. There's just so much to do." Stephanie nodded in understanding. Janet continued, "I don't like being late in the mornings, but I don't know what to do."

Stephanie sensed the conversation had gotten off on the right foot this time; together, they began to brainstorm ideas for resolving the situation.

With her choice to reflect on the situation, Stephanie gave herself the opportunity to look honestly at what was getting in the way of successfully resolving her issue with Janet. The act of

ATTITUDES FOR REFLECTION

John Dewey, the renowned educationalist, was a strong advocate of reflection and its ability to educate us. He believed the following attitudes formed a robust foundation for the practice of reflection:

Empathy for the circumstances and situations others face.

Open-mindedness to alternative points of view.

Curiosity about why and how things happen.

Self-awareness of one's thoughts, feelings, attitudes, and intentions.

Patience with ourselves and others' mistakes and struggles.

Courage to take risks, even when afraid.

Openness to feedback from others.

reflection always offers us the opportunity to stop and observe ourselves. It may take both patience and multiple attempts to resolve a situation, but without reflection's self-observation, it's difficult to know what to change or adapt.

Summary

➤ Reflection is an important tool for self-awareness; reflection requires taking the time to critically consider past situations.

➤ If we don't pause to reflect, we increase the probability of repeating past mistakes rather than learning from them.

➤ If you're not in the habit of reflecting, it may help you to think about reflection as a structured activity rather than a series of casual thoughts.

➤ Use the following questions to help yourself reflect:

1. What were your basic feelings, attitudes, and intentions in this situation?

2. What, if anything, did you say that you shouldn't have? What, if anything, did you *not* say that you should have?

3. What will you do differently next time?

CHAPTER 4

SIX RULES FOR THE ROAD

No matter how tough the terrain, smart people are *central players*—individuals committed to facing whatever situations they find themselves in from powerful points of view. We have observed six common rules for the road that they live by; each rule represents a facet of the personal responsibility that central players bring to their experience at work. After each rule we pose three questions designed to help you reflect on your own degree of personal responsibility in the workplace.

RULE 1: ENJOY THE JOURNEY

Central players are realists who are honest about their circumstances but don't easily succumb to workplace pessimism. They aren't lollygagging around waiting for work to get better! While central players may hope that difficult situations get resolved, or that the pressures of their job lessen, they aren't caught up in magical thinking—i.e., believing that one day they will miraculously have enough time and resources to get everything done perfectly. Rather, central players understand that they personally have the power to shape their approach to work so that they can enjoy the journey now rather than later.

Enjoying the journey means not wasting energy thinking about everything that *isn't* when your life is so full of everything that *is*. For example, imagine it's your first day back from a great vacation with friends or family. You're at work—and wishing you weren't. You long for the return of that relaxed, carefree vacation feeling: "If only I was retired in Hawaii.... If only I won the lottery.... If only I had a job that was less stressful, clients that were less demanding...." And so on. Wake up—this is it!

Smart people may have similar thoughts on their first day back, but instead of becoming miserable by dwelling on what isn't, they take an alternative route: they focus their attention on where they are, what they are doing, and how they might infuse their work with positive energy. "The vacation was really fun, but it's over now, so how can I make today a better workday?"

If you continually daydream about how you would rather be *there* rather than *here*, doing *that* rather than *this*, you are not living the life that is in front of you! We only have one life. What a waste it would be to endlessly rehearse only to discover the show is then over!

Ask yourself:

1. How much of your time at work is spent wishing you were somewhere else, doing something different? (Warning: if you spend one hour a day wishing you were somewhere else, by retirement age you would have wasted a year and a half!)

2. If, as you approached the end of your life, you were magically granted an extra eighteen months, how would you spend it? Would you would waste time wishing you were somewhere else or would you enjoy every moment?

3. What would you have to do to be more focused on what you're doing *right now*?

RULE 2: INVENT MEANINGFUL CONTEXTS

Because central players are unwilling to put off their satisfaction until later—and because they realize they can't change many of the irksome aspects of work (interruptions, deadlines, policies, etc.)—central players choose to view their circumstances through a meaningful context.

Focusing on a meaningful context can instantly change how we relate to even the most trying of circumstances. For example, in the wake of the 9/11 tragedy, many ordinary people who had lost loved ones chose a context of love and compassion over one of hate and revenge; e.g., some of the bereaved started charity groups to help bridge cultural divides and worked to build schools for children, particularly children in Muslim countries.

Less wrenching but still significant context possibilities present themselves to us every day in the workplace—if we choose to take them.

INVENT MEANINGFUL CONTEXTS

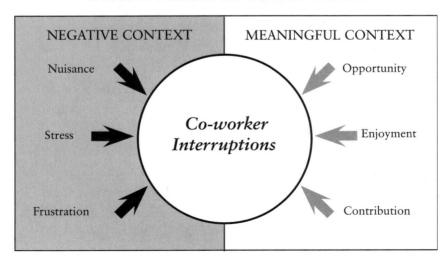

CASE STUDY: Gillian and Interruptions

Gillian, a senior salesperson for a large cable company, disliked being continually peppered by questions from the newcomers to the sales team. While she was the oldest and most seasoned person in the department, her responsibilities were similarly huge, and these continual interruptions, though well-intentioned, were annoying —Gillian would cringe every time she received an email or voicemail from a coworker who wanted to pick her brains about an account, a client, a policy, etc.

Gillian was asked to present a report on her key accounts at the national sales meeting. After her presentation, before she could leave the stage, an audience member grabbed the microphone and said, "I want to take this opportunity to thank Gillian for all the valuable advice she has given me over the months." Gillian nodded her thanks and was about to walk off the stage when the audience member continued, "I know that we're all very busy, but Gillian is not only accommodating, she's wise, and whenever I talk to her I feel that I'm getting the straight story. Thank you for sharing your time, knowledge and experience—and always saying it like it is." There was an immediate burst of applause; many of the group rose to their feet in appreciation. Gillian was shocked, embarrassed, and deeply moved. She had had no idea that she was making such a difference!

After the conference, Gillian reflected on how she had allowed herself to see her coworkers' questions as annoying interruptions to her job. Her new knowledge that her assistance was having a tremendous positive impact on others convinced Gillian to change her context. Now, instead of viewing each inquiry as an annoying interruption, she saw inquiries instead as opportunities to guide and coach. She decided to view each inquiry from now on as a validation of her expertise, straightforward style, and no-nonsense approach.

Ask yourself:

1. What negative contexts do you have at work about:
   - Your coworkers?
   - Your manager?
   - Your job?
   - Your customers?

2. What positive aspects can you find in any of the above situations?

3. How can you turn those positive aspects into a meaningful context?

RULE 3: CHOOSE CHOICE

Every day we make choices about how we behave in the many different situations we face. The default response is to react—to simply go along with whatever attitude, emotion, or behavior is evoked by the moment. For example: if you hear a loud noise behind you, you react by immediately turning around; if you see a box in the road, you react by instinctively swerving to avoid it.

Reacting helps us stay safe in many situations, but there are often times at work when reacting isn't useful—in fact, there are times at work when a knee-jerk response would be much better interrupted than expressed! For example, if a client calls you asking to move the delivery date on a project up two weeks, you might react without thinking and say indignantly, "That's impossible—and not what we agreed to!"

However, when we react like this, we aren't choosing our response, we're letting our response choose us. Smart people take a moment to choose how they will respond, rather than simply reacting to a situation.

Choosing what we say and do counters the resentment and negativity that can so easily dominate our mood at work. There are many things that we can't control at work, but no matter how busy, frazzled, or stressed we are, we always have the option to choose choice.

Ask yourself:

1. In what situations do you typically react without choosing? Is it related to a specific person, task, or circumstance?

2. Are you willing to stay silent for ten seconds the next time this situation occurs?

3. Regardless of who's at fault or who's to blame, would you be willing to *choose* your response in this situation rather than react?

RULE 4: DON'T BELIEVE EVERYTHING YOU THINK

Imagine standing in line at your local supermarket in the express lane. After glancing at the tabloids ("Headless Bloodhound Sniffs Out Hoffa Remains!"), you notice that the person in front of you has a basket overflowing with grocery items. In fact, you silently count fifteen items, five more than is allowed in the express lane—and that's if you only count the six-pack of soda as one item! You wonder if you should say something, but decide it would seem too petty. But for a full three minutes—until the person has finally left the store—you are obsessed with a silent, senseless conversation with yourself about this "illegal" item count.

We can become so involved in our world of manufactured thoughts that we fail to discriminate if they are useful. Do they empower us? Some do—some can be life-preserving for us, such as, "Uh-oh, here comes the boss, better put the GameBoy away!" Or, "Better slow down, this car is never going to make it over that barricade!" Or, "Dry your hands and turn off the power *before* you check the 220V circuit." But others, like the ones in the express lane example above, are not particularly useful.

We once encountered a teacher who demonstrated very clearly that we all have the power to observe our thoughts. At the beginning of his lecture he asked us to stay perfectly quiet for a moment and listen to the little voice that we had talking to us inside our heads (feel free to try this in the safety of your own home). After a few seconds, he asked us if we heard the little voice talking to us. To people who looked confused or uncertain he suggested that their little voice was probably saying something like, "What little voice? I don't hear a little voice. What's he talking about?" As the penny dropped, the looks of confusion on the students' faces slowly turned to amusement.

He then asked us who it was that was *listening* to those thoughts. Obviously it was us. But it was a part of us, he explained, that is able to observe and listen with a judicious perspective, if we so choose. Our teacher believed this was particularly significant knowledge given that our minds often take the doom and gloom approach to reality. Rather than just unquestioningly believing every thought we have, he suggested we implement some quality control over the negative assumptions, unconstructive opinions, and discouraging judgments that we sometimes make about both ourselves and others.

Ask yourself:

1. Are there any recurring thoughts that have overstayed their welcome in your mind?

2. Do these type of thoughts ever help you resolve a problem?

3. What can you do to move on from them?

RULE 5: FIND SUCCESS IN FAILURE

We all experience failure at work. For most of us, not meeting a deadline, not quite completing a project, or not reaching some other goal is accompanied by a raft of excuses that help protect us from the unpalatable truth—we failed! We blame circumstances, management, other departments, interruptions, morale, market trends—even the weather!—but in doing so we miss an important opportunity to grow and learn.

You may be reading this and thinking that the other department *was* to blame for a missed deadline. Why should you take the rap when it wasn't your fault? Central players answer this question by looking at the situation from an entirely different perspective. Central players see failure as an opportunity for discovery rather than a chance to apportion blame. Regardless of who was at fault, central players know that if they focus their attention on who should get nailed rather than what *they* could have done differently, they stop being a central player and become a victim.

In *Juice: The Creative Fuel That Drives World-Class Inventors* (2004), Evan I. Schwartz explained the importance of failure very clearly

> Failure is the rule rather than the exception, and every failure contains information. One of the most misleading lessons imparted by those who have reached their

goal is that the ones who win are the ones who perse-
vere. Not always. If you keep trying without learning
why you failed, you'll probably fail again and again.
Perseverance must be accompanied by the embrace of
failure. Failure is what moves you forward. Listen to
failure.

Failure is a wonderful opportunity for discovery because it
makes visible what was previously completely unseen. As soon as
something stops working correctly we are forced to become more
aware of how it functions. Think about the last time your computer had a glitch or your car broke down. Up until the point of
failure you were probably unaware of the mechanics and engi-
neering at play; however, once the computer or car stopped
working, you became excruciatingly aware of how it was sup-
posed to function—and were forced to figure out why it wasn't.
(Kicking the tires of your car or blaming your laptop manufacturer is a natural reaction, but spending any longer than a few seconds on this wastes time, creates stress, and does nothing to fix
the problem.) Likewise, failing in an endeavor offers us the
opportunity to understand and improve upon what has previously
gone unnoticed.

From childhood on we grow as a result of our failures. We
learn about heat by touching the stove: ouch! We walk and fall
over: ouch! The ouch-and-learn process only ends when we begin
to blame others rather than look for improvements within.

Ask yourself:

1. How often do you blame others or the circumstances?
    Frequently, occasionally, or rarely?

2. How often do you see yourself as the victim of other
    people's failures? Frequently, occasionally, or rarely?

3. Is there a relationship between your answers to question 1 and question 2?

RULE 6: CULTIVATE OPTIMISM

One of the strongest underlying sentiments in many companies is that nothing and no one can make a difference: the service improvement initiative didn't really improve service; the employee reward program didn't improve morale even a little bit; the reorganization just made everyone crazy—and now everything's worse!

With cynicism so rampant, having an upbeat and positive outlook could easily get you labeled a Pollyanna out of touch with reality and naïve to the way things really work. Like a strong river current, a negative company culture can pull you in and sweep you downstream until, without you even realizing it, your optimistic self gets dragged down into the depths and you, too, become part of the problem.

Smart people don't succumb to this *Invasion of the Body Snatchers* condition. It's not that smart people are naïve or out of touch with reality; rather, smart people believe (even when they have little or no evidence to support it) that something good is always a possible outcome, even from the most trying of circumstances. This faith in beneficial possibilities creates a healthier, more balanced outlook.

CASE STUDY: Jack and the Longshoremen

Jack is a senior executive at a large freight and shipping line. A no-nonsense, hard-headed character, Jack had come up through the ranks and had been a union representative himself until moving to the other side of the negotiating table and joining management. Jack's work environment was usually pretty harsh—filled with labor disputes, dockyard politics, and schedules that changed with the tides.

Jack's company was engaged in a series of frustrating negotiations with the union regarding contract renewal. They'd reached an impasse: both parties had dug in and refused to budge. The dominant attitude of Jack's peers, all seasoned pros, was pessimism. They had been here before and it never boded well. They were all set for the inevitable work stoppage. The containerized freight would not be moved from the vessels to the dockside and vice versa. Since ships couldn't leave without their freight, inbound ships wouldn't have available berths. It was going to be a nightmare.

Jack's attitude was different. "I've been in this business for years," said Jack. "There's a lot of bad history and both sides bring it to the negotiation table. Everyone believes that nothing we say or do is going to change anything, so why bother? But if I adopt that same attitude then a bad outcome is *guaranteed*. I have no idea what will happen tomorrow at the meeting—there's a lot at stake. But all I can do is walk in and sit down and listen with an open mind—and not let all the bad history rob us of a settlement. There is an answer, I know there is, and it's my job to find it."

Jack did find it. By focusing on the possibility of a resolution instead of just giving in to the deeply entrenched negative opinions each side had for the other, Jack snatched victory from the jaws of defeat. The dispute was resolved and a full-blown strike narrowly avoided. Afterwards, Jack told us, "I was shocked how everyone in the room was really fighting for failure ... the way questions were asked, the way answers were given—it was like an echo from every other meeting that had never worked out. In situations like this one it's hard to keep an even keel, but focusing on what's possible, that's what it takes if you're going to succeed."

Ask yourself:

1. How much optimism do you bring to your job and workplace? A lot, an average amount, or very little?

2. If you bring very little optimism to your job, what other attitude(s) would you have to give up to increase your optimism?

3. What could your personal motivation be for increasing your optimism at work?

Summary

➤ Smart people don't waste energy on wishing things were different; instead, smart people focus their attention on where they are, what they are doing, and how they can infuse the present moment with positive energy.

➤ While you may not be able to change all of the annoying aspects of everyday work life—interruptions, deadlines, meetings, etc.—a meaningful context can instantly change how you relate to, and think about, even the most trying of circumstances.

➤ Reacting is a natural response, but not always the most beneficial one; by taking the time to choose how you are going to respond you both take responsibility for the energy you project and become less susceptible to workplace negativity.

➤ We manufacture thoughts all day long; by recognizing that thoughts sometimes aren't based on true perspectives, you become better able to discriminate between those that are empowering and those that increase stress and misunderstanding.

➤ Failure provides us with valuable opportunities to grow and learn; however, you lose these opportunities if you're always busy assigning blame. By ignoring your role in a failure, you never ask yourself what you could do differently next time.

➤ Optimism doesn't mean being out of touch with workplace reality, it means considering things from a balanced perspective and being willing to find the silver lining in even the most trying of circumstances.

PART 2

PRESSURE: SMART PEOPLE CREATE TOMORROW TODAY

Energy is the essence of life. Every day you decide how you're going to use it by knowing what you want and what it takes to reach that goal, and by maintaining focus.

—Oprah Winfrey

CHAPTER 5

THE POWER OF CLOSURE

Imagine that it's Monday morning and you've just had a wonderful weekend. You successfully achieved the much sought after perfect balance of time with your family, social engagements, and getting the necessary chores done. You spent time with people you love, curled up with a good book, watched a movie, ran a few errands, and even got in a little exercise.

The alarm rings and you arise, rested, happy, and full of energy. Onward to your morning ablutions! But when you pick up the toothpaste tube you realize that there's nothing left—at this point, only a steamroller could coax another dollop of toothpaste out of the tube. You've been meaning to buy some more but you've been so darn busy …

Okay, no big deal. You quickly move on to the next stop in your morning routine, the shower. No shampoo. "Who used it up and didn't get more?" you mutter as you step into the shower. But what the heck, you can wash your hair with soap. Stepping out of the shower, you make a mental note to stop by the store *today* for both toothpaste and shampoo—and now that you're thinking about it, you're running low on toilet paper, too!

It's time to get dressed. You open your closet (*not* one that would be featured on The Home Channel's "how to organize a closet" segment!) and are confronted by chaos: shoes strewn everywhere, clothes hung wherever—even a few boxes of old tax records jammed in, too! Carefully stepping over the boxes, you fish out the perfect jacket for today's big meeting.

Unfortunately, it appears you forgot to take the jacket to the cleaners to have that ugly coffee stain removed. "Oh well," you think, "I'll just have to make do with my old one. It's a bit small, but no other choice now." You add yet another mental note to your list: take jacket to cleaners.

With just enough time to grab some breakfast before you head off to work, you hurry into the kitchen and notice (once again) the burnt-out light bulb you've been meaning to replace for the past two weeks. Another mental note.

A quick cup of coffee and you're off. But where are the car keys? After much searching—and ranting—you find them in a desk drawer buried under the letter from the IRS you've been meaning to respond to. Oops. Yes, another mental note!

At last you arrive at work. As you approach your desk you see a stack of phone messages from the previous week, still unreturned; a fat pile of papers spilling across the desk; the Chinese takeout you forgot to throw out on Friday. Yuck!

THE PRINCIPLE OF DIMINISHED ENERGY

What has happened to all that energy you had when you woke up? Well if you are like most people, it's probably rather diminished at this point—if not altogether gone! Even reading this story, did you find yourself getting tired and maybe even a bit cranky? Were you thinking, "STOP! I can't take any more"?

This example illustrates the powerful point that a lack of closure diminishes energy. In other words, it's often the unfinished or incomplete little things—personal or business—that reduce our energy level and distract us from the tasks at hand. And, as the Encarta dictionary defines it, energy is "liveliness; the ability or power to work or make an effort; a supply or source of power; the capacity of a body or system to do work."

Closure Generates Energy

The converse of "lack of closure diminishes energy" is "closure *creates* energy." When things are finished—even very little things—we feel a renewed sense of energy. For example:

- How do you feel when you put a check next to an item on your to-do list?

- How do you feel when you get to the end of a project you have been working on?

- How do you feel when you finally communicate something to a friend or coworker that you've been putting off for a long time?

Jean, a school teacher: *I had been meaning to make an appointment to take my car in for its 30,000 mile checkup for two weeks. Every day I found myself thinking "I really need to call and scheddule this." Of course other things came up, and I never got round to it. Finally, I just made myself sit down, pick up the phone dial, and make the appointment. I am almost embarrassed at how much relief and satisfaction I felt at getting this one small thing done.*

Smart people know that the more closure they create at work (and at home), the more energy they have to put into accomplishing those things that matter most.

WHAT FINISHED FEELS LIKE

To bring this idea home, take some time to complete the following exercise:

Step 1: Write down two business and two personal items that you intended, or wanted, to get done in the past few days but didn't. For example:

> Return a phone call.
>
> Write an e-mail about the upcoming trip.
>
> Take clothes to the cleaners.
>
> Replace a light bulb in garage.

Now take a moment to think about how you feel about not having done those items. Write the feeling next to the item associated with it, and be as specific as you can. (In other words, don't just write down "good" or "bad," write down particular feelings—e.g. sad, frustrated, upset, etc. You may find it helpful to reference the Name That Feeling! tool of chapter 2.)

Step 2: Write down two business and two personal items that you intended to do in the past few days and *did* get done. How does it feel to have completed these items? Again, write the feeling next to the item associated with it, being as specific as you can.

Notice the difference between the two lists? While the little things you leave unfinished may drain you of energy, the flipside is equally true. Bringing things to closure generates energy and gives you a greater ability to focus on the tasks at hand.

Strategize Closure with the 4-D Plan

How do you know when something is incomplete rather than just not done? Both from observing ourselves and working with other people we've found that lack of closure has a very particular feeling—a nagging, annoying feeling. Lack of closure has frustration built into it—one of its recurring themes is: "I intended to do this but somehow keep not doing it." On the other hand, something that you want to do but haven't gotten around to yet—but have a specific plan to achieve—rests a lot easier on the mind. Although few people finish *everything* they've planned to do in a day, it's still possible to leave work at the end of the day with a sense of completion and closure. The key is to strategize closure by using one of the four D's on all of your to-do items.

Do It Now

The phone rings: it's your bigger client asking you to email them a proposal for a new project. You put the phone down and spend the next hour putting together the information they need and then email it off. Check that one off your list! Item done, closure achieved, energy generated. What a gift it would be if every item we had to get done could get whisked from in-box to out-box so quickly…. But since that's just not so, there are still three other ways to achieve a sense of closure.

Do It Later

Although the top of the closure heap is immediately getting an item done, the next best thing is to schedule doing it later. Setting a specific date and/or time for working on a task frees up the energy you would otherwise use thinking about doing it. The key to doing it later is to write it down—and we don't mean on the back of a napkin or old burrito wrapper! Rather, have a system in place, whether paper or electronic, that lets you track what items you plan to do on a given day.

Delegate It

Delegating an item gets it moving toward completion but doesn't require you to be the one who takes care of it. The best items for delegation are routine duties, tasks that aren't really up your alley, or activities that you're just plain bad at! Remember: delegation isn't abdication. You may have given the item to someone else to complete, but you still have the responsibility to ensure it is done.

Dump It

Items that you plan to do but keep shirking are a big energy drain. It can be empowering to just let some of these items go. Although they might be good ideas, you may simply lack the time, resources, or commitment necessary to make them happen. Here's a useful tip: if you have transferred a particular item ten times in your date book (from one day to the next and so on), then you need to reflect on how dedicated you are to actually getting it done. One answer may be that the task is too big to manage and you need to break it down into more doable steps (see chapter 8: The Habits of Action). Alternatively, it may be time for you to admit to yourself that the item is unlikely to ever get done—in which case, it's a candidate for abandonment. Abandoning an item generates energy from the closure that comes of consciously letting go and moving on.

Smart people have a finely tuned sense about when to do, delegate, or dump an item. What smart people avoid is the dreaded fifth D: denial. Although pretending an item doesn't need to be dealt with when it does may appear to save you time in the short term, in the long term it can be a massive energy drain. Denying what you need to do is the anti-closure.

Bring Some Closure to Your Computer

A study by Accounttemps in 2003 found that office workers spend an average of six weeks per year looking for things. If you combine this with the fact that 70 percent of Americans use computers, it's not hard to see that the computer is one of the primary places we spend our time and energy searching for things. To organize and help bring some closure to your computer, follow these five steps:

Step 1: Set Up a Logical Filing System

Try to mirror your paper filing system; the more your computer folders resemble your paper folders the easier it will be for you to both find and file documents. Create a "working" file to hold anything you are currently working on or need to be able to access easily and put it on your desktop.

Step 2: Organize and Update the Bookmarks on Your Browser

Just as you may have random files floating around on your hard drive, you more than likely have a ton of bookmarks that aren't organized in any particular way. Most web browsers offer a variety of bookmark organizing features; go to your browser's "bookmarks" to delete dead bookmarks and make new folders to organize all of your various bookmarks.

Step 3: Clean Up Your Hard Drive

Because computer memory has increased so much over the past few years, hard disk storage usually isn't a big issue these days. As a result, you may have developed the bad habit of using your computer as an information dumping ground—whether the information is still relevant or not. Here are a few ways to clean up your hard drive:

- Delete any old drafts of documents that have since been updated or are no longer useful.

- Eliminate files that contain duplicate materials.

- Dump files that are so old the information in them is outdated.

One caution: If you need to keep files for legal reasons, print them out on paper and keep a hard copy and/or create a special "legal" folder for them on your computer.

Step 4: Take Control of Your Email

Start by going through your mailbox and deleting all old messages you no longer need (as well as any spam that may still be hanging around). Because you probably have enough room on your computer to keep old email, you may be tempted to skip this step. However, we find that the more current and up-to-date your email, the less time you'll spend searching for what you need.

Step 5: Establish an Email Filing System

Set up a system that makes it quick and easy to find past emails. You can use various ways to archive and prioritize messages. One method is setting up your email folders the same way you organize your work. (For example, if you organize your work by client, set up your email folders by client name; if you organize by product, set up your folders by product name; etc.) When new emails arrive, don't let them linger in your mailbox hoping they will read themselves! For every incoming message you receive, take at least one of the following four actions:

- Reply immediately whenever possible.

- Delete the message.

- Forward as appropriate.

- File the message in the appropriate folder.

Finally, don't fall into the trap of ignoring incoming messages. Anything you try to ignore becomes a loose end—and consequently a big energy drain.

Summary

➤ It's often the unfinished or incomplete little things around us that create a lack of closure and rob us of energy.

➤ Smart people focus on creating closure at work (and at home) so that they have the energy necessary to accomplish important tasks and goals.

➤ Although you won't finish everything you've planned to do every day, you can still leave work experiencing a sense of completion and closure.

➤ Strategize closure by using the 4-D Plan: do it now, do it later, delegate it, or dump it.

➤ Denying an item needs to be dealt with may save time in the short run but will lead to a massive energy drain in the long run.

➤ Computers are a big area where lack of closure lurks. Bring closure to your computer by working on five key areas: set up a logical filing system, organize and update your bookmarks, clean out your hard drive, take control of your email, and establish an email filing system.

CHAPTER 6

WORK HAPPIER, NOT HARDER

How many hours do you expect to work over the course of your lifetime? On average, Americans will spend more than 80,000 hours at work! The question is, what will be the quality of those hours? Will they be spent in frustration, disappointment, and regret? Or will they be spent in making meaningful contributions, forging close relationships, and achieving goals? Smart people know that learning to work happier, not harder not only decreases the pressure and stress they feel today, but also increases their productivity and satisfaction at work now and in the future. Smart people know that at the heart of working happier, not harder is striking a work-life balance that reflects their goals, values, and gifts.

AIM FOR THE FUTURE

Earl Nightingale, founder of Nightingale Conant Audio Company and a pioneer in the personal development industry, once said, "People with goals succeed because they know where they are going.... It's as simple as that." In fact, it's hard to find a business, self-help, or spiritual book today that doesn't discuss the importance and power of setting goals. But as effective as goal-setting is, in reality we still spend more time planning a dinner party than we do planning our work and life goals. Smart people know that while achieving goals has its challenges the place to start is setting effective goals.

Write Your Goals Down

According to Lee Iacocca, the former chairman of GM, "The discipline of writing something down is the first step toward making it happen." For many people, the simple act of putting pen to paper and articulating their goals is enough to spur them to action. Writing your goals down provides you with a point of reference for the future, gives your subconscious mind a project to work on, and increases the odds that you will actually reach your goal. Goals that you don't write down may be good ideas, but they often fail to move from your mind to the real world. One poll by ehappylife.com in 2003 found that only 25 percent of people write their goals down.

Accentuate the Positive

Goals that are stated as a positive step towards something you want are more effective than those that focus on what you want to avoid or remove. For example, Beth Tabakin, a therapist specializing in weight management, asks her clients to set a goal for what they want to weigh (i.e., "I want to weigh 125 pounds by January 1st"), rather than a goal for the weight they want to lose (i.e., "I want to lose 20 pounds by January 1st"). By focusing on the constructive aspect of the goal, you provide your subconscious mind with a positive pathway to follow. Dr. Tabakin also encourages her clients to change the way they talk about their progress. Instead of saying, "I lost a pound this week"—which

VALUES ◄ **GOALS** ► TO-DOs

Written
Positive
Challenging
Comprehensive
Specific

suggests that you might find the pound again sometime in the future—Dr. Tabakin suggests rephrasing this into: "I got rid of a pound this week." These changes in language are deceptively simple but can have a powerful impact on the achievement of goals.

Go For Goals That Stretch You

There's an old proverb that goes something like this: you don't teach a six-foot man to swim by putting him in water ten-feet deep, because he'll just drown. But if you put the same man in seven feet of water, he'll become a better swimmer. Goals that are achievable but just a little bit bigger than those we've achieved previously stretch us to go beyond our comfort zone. And if you shoot for the moon and miss, you'll still hit the stars.

CASE STUDY: Steve and the Black T-Shirt

One of our friends is a chiropractor and an avid runner. For the past twenty-one years he has competed in a cross-country foot race in Northern California. In all the years he had run the race, his best finish was sixty-fifth when he was 36 years old. At age 54, Steve set a goal to run the race and win a coveted black t-shirt, awarded to the first thirty-five runners to reach the finish line. "This race has really captured my heart. I love the ups and downs of the course and I have no fear of falling," explained Steve. "I always wanted to be among the winners and it's a race that favors my body type and my willingness to take risks. I thought the goal of coming in thirty-fifth—or better—was a stretch but doable."

In order to achieve his goal Steve trained for a year, running about fifty miles a week—33 percent more miles than his usual running practice. On the day of the race, many of Steve's friends and family were stationed along the course to cheer him on and provide moral support.

Fifteen hundred people started out at the beginning of the race. At the finish line, Steve came in fortieth—five shy of his goal but twenty-five places better than his best previous race. He came in only twenty seconds behind the thirty-fifth person. After the race, he wrote a letter to all of his friends and family. "I want you to know," wrote Steve, "that I suffered no disappointment whatsoever. It may be difficult to believe but it's true. I chased one of my demons for almost a year, an unfulfilled childhood dream of athletic brilliance and heroic effort. Sunday's performance was heroic. On that day I could not have done more. It was my greatest athletic moment ever and its effect plays on all the levels of my being. It will be with me forever."

Make Your Goals Specific

What you can measure, you can manage. When setting goals, it's important to identify both a clearly defined outcome and a specific timeline so that you know not only when you've achieved the goal but also how you are doing along the way. For example, let's say your goal is to improve your time management skills at work. Not a bad idea—but how will you know that you've achieved it given that you haven't attached any specific criteria to the goal? And when are you planning to do this? Now, next week, or next year? Compare this with the goal to improve your time management skills by practicing time-planning every day and doing a daily to-do and priority list. See the difference? The first goal is general, undefined, and passive. The second goal is stated in a way that shouts out for action.

Many people resist specific goals because they fear being stuck with what they created. Keep in mind that you can change or adjust your goals—and that doing so doesn't represent a failure. Goals should be organic, living creations rather than stagnant entities. As you progress toward a particular goal, the circumstances surrounding it may change. Making appropriate adjustments to its timeline and specific aspects can be a critical factor in its successful accomplishment.

Create Goals for All Areas of Life

Whether short-term or long-term, unusual or mundane, easy or challenging, smart people know that setting goals in different areas of life helps to ensure a healthy balance of interests and achievements. To get your goal-setting muscles in motion, use the following categories for inspiration. Brainstorm some goals you would like to create by writing down anything that comes to mind. Don't edit yourself when writing—often you can discover important yet hidden dreams by giving your mind full creative rein. After you've finished writing you can then edit out anything that isn't realistic.

Health and Fitness
>   Nutrition, exercise, weight, medical.

Family and Relationship
>   Marriage, dating, family, friendships.

Financial
>   Personal finances, income, investment, paying off debts, budgeting, charity, real estate.

Creativity
>   Art, music, writing, dance, acting, singing, performing.

Career
>   Job promotion, getting hired, entrepreneurial activities.

Sports and Recreation
>   Boating, golfing, tennis, hiking, biking, running, vacations.

Personal Development
>   Education, spirituality, therapy, self-awareness, time management, organization.

Home Improvement
>   Remodeling, refinancing, gardening.

FROM YOUR GOALS, VALUES COME

A poll conducted by the Center for a New American Dream in 2004 revealed that a staggering 93 percent of those surveyed felt that Americans focus too much on working and making money and not enough on family and community. In this same survey, when asked what phrase best describes the American Dream, 86 percent chose the phrase "getting more of what matters in life" over "more is better."

Your values are what matter most in your life. Regularly reviewing and renewing your commitment to your values can both help you withstand the day-to-day pressures of life and help you create meaningful contexts for whatever is going on around you (for more information on the importance of creating meaningful contexts, see chapter 4).

The prevailing point of view is that if you know what your values are, you can then find goals that are the appropriate expressions of those values. We believe the opposite makes more practical sense: you can discover your values by looking at your goals. Smart people know their goals are a good indication of what really matters to them and they make sure that their goals and values are consistent.

The Core Four

In *The Nude Ethicist* (2004), Olive Gallagher talks about the four core ethical values. She says, "The list of values we can choose from to enhance the quality of our lives is quite long.... The list of *ethical* values each of us can choose from, to include and honor in our actions, is short, there are only four: Honesty. Integrity. Respect. Fairness." However, beyond these four core ethical values, we all also have personal values that reflect our individual commitments.

Your Personal Values

While core values determine how you function in and relate to society, personal values help define you as an individual and guide your choices about how you spend your time and whom you spend it with.

What are your five most important personal values? Take a moment to write them down. (If you need a brain-booster, go through the Personal Values List below. And remember: you don't need to include the core four of honesty, integrity, respect, and fairness—they're assumed.)

```
┌─────────────────────────────────────────────────┐
│              PERSONAL VALUES LIST               │
│  This is a partial list of personal values; use it to help │
│  clarify your own values.                       │
│                                                 │
│                                                 │
│   Achievement    Humor           Perseverance   │
│                                                 │
│   Appreciation   Imagination     Philanthropy   │
│                                                 │
│   Balance        Independence    Reliability    │
│                                                 │
│   Boldness       Joy             Resolve        │
│                                                 │
│   Compassion     Justice         Satisfaction   │
│                                                 │
│   Creativity     Kindness        Self-Reliance  │
│                                                 │
│   Discovery      Knowledge       Teamwork       │
│                                                 │
│   Duty           Leadership      Thankfulness   │
│                                                 │
│   Efficiency     Learning        Thoughfulness  │
│                                                 │
│   Excellence     Making a        Understanding  │
│                  difference                     │
│   Flexibility                    Usefulness     │
│                  Mindfulness                    │
│   Freedom                        Valor          │
│                  Neatness                       │
│   Fun                            Vision         │
│                  Open-                          │
│   Generosity     Mindedness      Warmth         │
│                                                 │
│   Growth                         Willingness    │
│                  Optimism                       │
│   Harmony                        Zest for life  │
│                                                 │
└─────────────────────────────────────────────────┘
```

Work Values

Work values inform the choices you make in your work life, including how you interact with your coworkers, what projects you volunteer to take on, and what career moves you make. Take a look at the following list of work values and assign each one a color—green, yellow, or red—based on the following:

Green

These work values are a must; they provide you with the greatest sense of happiness and satisfaction at work.

Yellow

These are the work values that you appreciate but aren't in the make-or-break category for your happiness at work.

Red

These are the work values that would contribute to your being *unhappy* at work.

WORK VALUES LIST

Contributing to the lives of others or society as a whole

Working as part of a team

Working by myself

Independently determining the planning and execution of my work

Making a lot of money

Security and stability

Creative expression at work

Managing other people

Managing myself

Learning and growing in my job

Using my people skills

Traveling as a part of my job

Not traveling as a part of my job

Being in a fast-paced, high-energy work environment

Being in a quiet, calm, and peaceful work setting

Personal satisfaction in getting my job done well

Finding my work engaging; being absorbed in my work

Working outdoors; being around nature

Competing against others

Working with the public

Having very little interaction with the public

Having an influence on others individually and/or society as a whole

Using my physical capabilities

Using my intellectual capabilities

Using my analytical skills, including attention to detail

Working on a fixed schedule with fixed hours

Working on a flexible schedule to meet my changing personal needs

Review the items that you marked as a green; these are your core work values. How does your current work life compare? Are you working in a job that helps fulfill and express these work values? If not, what could you do to change that? The more you can connect your goals at work—both long-term and short-term—to your core work values, the more satisfaction you will have.

CONNECTING YOUR VALUES AND GOALS

Think about some of the goals that you identified earlier in the chapter. Do your goals and work values connect with each other? For example, if one of your goals for this quarter is to "have a team-building event off-site" and one of your values is "working with others on a team," there's an obvious connection. However, in some cases the connection may be more subtle; for example, if one of your values is "making a lot of money" and you see that the team-building event will lead to a stronger, more profitable company, then the goal still—albeit in a less direct way—supports that value. When looking at your goals ask yourself, "What, in essence, will I get by achieving this goal? Does it connect with one of my personal or work values?"

Is there a value that you hold deeply which has no goals that support it? If so, why not develop a related goal? Do you have any goals that don't connect to any of your values? If so, why? Are they simply good ideas rather than authentic goals? Knowing and connecting your goals and values provides you with the clarity to make everyday decisions that are consistent with what is most important to you in life.

Your Best You

In his poem, "Two Tramps In Mud Time," Robert Frost wrote,

> "My object in living is to unite
> My avocation and my vocation
> As my two eyes make one in sight."

Deep in our hearts, many of us wish that our calling and what we do for a living could be one and the same—or at least a little closer together! Although this joining of avocation and vocation is a reality for some of us, for most of us it is not. Smart people strive to express their gifts at work because doing so helps close the gap between their avocation (calling) and their vocation (livelihood). The satisfaction you experience at work—and in life—comes from knowing, expressing, and living true to your most heartfelt and deepest gifts. Dana, a colleague of ours, put it this way:

> "Ever since I turned 40 a few years ago, I've been thinking about what the next part of my life will be about: How will I spend the time I have left? What difference do I want to make in the world? The first 40 years were taken up with the accomplishments I wanted to achieve. During a workshop, I had the realization that my true gift is creativity and that I really have an artistic spirit. My focus in the next part of my life is to express that creativity to the fullest of my abilities in all the different ways it manifests including in my job at work. Discovering this took a lot of pressure off and freed me up to begin to truly share my gifts in all areas of my life."

Size Really Doesn't Matter

Every one of us, regardless of our occupation, has deep and heartfelt gifts that are a unique contribution we alone can bring to work. However, sometimes we can't see how our gifts contribute to the larger whole, or we think our gifts aren't as valuable or noble as another's. For example, anyone familiar with the Miss America Pageant knows the "If you win, how would you use your crown to contribute to the world?" question. The answer is never small or mundane—usually it's something like, "I want to create world peace!" or "End hunger." While these are both beautiful and noble gifts, are they really any more important than what you have to contribute? We don't think so. If everyone at your place of work (and in the world) was in touch with, and truly expressing, their most heartfelt gifts, work—and the world—would be a very different place.

Because we get so caught up in the pursuit of goals and accomplishments, we can overlook the unique gifts we have to give. Never in the history of the world has their been, or will there ever be, another you. You may meet ten other people who feel they have the same gifts to give as you, but they will never express them in the same way. How you choose to give your gifts is a rich expression of who you are and can never be replicated by anyone else in quite the same way.

> **Luis, a Web site designer:** *I've always felt that one of my best gifts is helping people to communicate more effectively. In my work I use this gift to empower people to use the Internet to communicate their messages and achieve their goals.*

> **Elizabeth, VP of a nonprofit:** *I've always had a passion to support and work with people. Specifically, I like to create possibilities for people. One of my gifts is taking something big and figuring out how to get it done—not to prove what I can do but to help those around me see new possibilities. I like the teamwork of working with others to figure out how to do things.*

> **Erin, recruiter:** *My whole life I've been a very organized person. Often, when there's a big project, meeting, or conference at work that needs to be planned and coordinated, I'm the one my boss asks to handle it. I really enjoy it because I feel like I am a natural at this*

and it gives me a chance to shine at something I am
better at than almost anyone I know.

We all lead busy lives. We have more to do but less time and resources to do it with than ever before. In the face of this pressure, we must remember our gifts and gain nourishment from conscientiously expressing them every opportunity we get.

FINDING YOUR GIFTS

Imagine you are sitting in a restaurant when you hear familiar voices coming from a neighboring table. It's a group of your coworkers talking about the people they work with. Suddenly, you overhear your name. Making yourself as invisible as possible, you listen as they talk about the positive qualities you contribute at work.

1. Write down what you think you would hear your coworkers saying. *Warning:* positive qualities only!

2. Next, imagine you overhear a group of your friends talking about the qualities you bring to your friendships; add these to the list of your positive qualities.

3. Lastly, what have friends or family told you over the years that they appreciate about you? Which of your qualities do they praise and compliment?

4. When you think about or look at these qualities, do you notice a theme? Does a common thread jump out at you? Can you summarize it in a few words?

Summary

► Working happier, not harder is about spending the time you have at work on those goals and values that matter the most to you.

► Effective goals are written down, positive, challenging, specific, and in all areas of life.

► You can discover what many of your values are by looking at your goals.

► The four core ethical values are honesty, integrity, respect, and fairness.

► Your personal values guide your choices about how you spend your time and who you spend it with.

► Your work values inform the career choices you make and how you interact with those around you in the work environment.

► Your values and your goals need to be congruent and connected.

► You have unique gifts to give.

CHAPTER 7

IDEA TO ACCOMPLISHMENT

Being aware of your values, creating effective goals, and living true to your gifts will get you a long way toward experiencing a strong sense of accomplishment and achievement at work. Determining how you are going to spend your time each and every day is the critical last step in creating tomorrow today. As Peter Drucker, author of *The Effective Executive* (1966), has long espoused, it's not just doing things in the right way, it's doing the *right things* that really matters.

Smart people appreciate that by spending time every day on the right things they are consistently moving away from the frantic wheel-spinning of empty activity and toward the satisfaction of excellence and accomplishment.

THE 80/20 RELATIONSHIP AND YOU

Many people who are highly efficient are not very effective, and vice-versa. Efficiency is about doing a job well—in the right way, with an appropriate amount of effort, and in a timely manner. Effectiveness, on the other hand, is about doing the right job—the job that will make the biggest difference toward accomplishing your given objectives.

In the early 20th century, the Italian economist Vilfredo Pareto observed that 20 percent of citizens owned 80 percent of the wealth. Decades later, Joseph M. Juran, a leader in the quality control movement, borrowed Pareto's 80/20 discovery and adapted it to various business arenas. For example, Juran believed that 20 percent of defects caused 80 percent of quality problems; 20 percent of people do 80 percent of the work; and 80 percent of the reward comes from only 20 percent of the work. This 80/20 relationship has been applied to business in almost every domain, from sales to quality management.

Smart people use the 80/20 relationship to remind them to focus on the few items (the 20 percent) that matter most and will produce the most results (the 80 percent). Of all the things you do in your day, what is the 20 percent that matters most? What is the 20 percent that will produce 80 percent of the results you desire?

The Traditional ABC

In *CEO Logic: How to Think and Act Like a Chief Executive*, C. Ray Johnson wrote,

> Prioritizing is the answer to time management problems —not computers, efficiency experts, or matrix scheduling. You do not need to do work faster or to eliminate gaps in productivity to make better use of your time. You need to spend more time on the right things ...

Prioritizing allows you to determine what your 20 percent is so that you can make the smart choices about how to get the most out of the time you invest every day, every week, and every month.

Although there are many different methods of prioritizing to-do items, the most common one is the ABC method based on urgency:

A = Most urgent

B = Moderately urgent

C = Least urgent

However, the problem with following this system is that you end up always managing crises, putting out whichever fire is burning hottest at the moment. Even more significantly, this ABC method does not help you focus on doing the 20 percent of activities that move you the 80 percent toward achieving your goals.

ABC With a Twist

In *The Seven Habits of Highly Effective People* (1989), Stephen Covey made a distinction between things that were important to get done and things that were urgent to get done. With a nod to Mr. Covey, our ABC method distinguishes between things that are time-sensitive and goal-related. Items that are time-sensitive require immediate action or attention; time-sensitive items often have tight deadlines or represent crises that demand action on the spot. Goal-related items, on the other hand, are actions that move you closer to achieving your goals. In our ABC method of prioritizing to-do items, A, B, and C rankings are based on each item's connection to your goals.

A = Both goal-related and time-sensitive

B = Goal-related but not time-sensitive

C = Not goal-related (may or may not be time-sensitive)

Make Way for the A's

A items are those to-do items that are both strongly goal-related *and* time-sensitive. They provide a sense of accomplishment because they move you toward achieving your objectives and at the same time have a pressing quality about them. A items often involve a deadline, contract, or problem that needs immediate solving. Moreover, A items can bring a great deal of satisfaction on two fronts: first, you feel good about getting something done that is important; second, you get the relief of moving it off your action list!

B's Are Key

B items are goal-related but aren't time-sensitive. B items often involve strategy, planning, and organization. Taking action on B items would make a big difference, but because B items don't have any urgency or time constraint associated with them, they often sit untouched for weeks or months—sometimes even years.

> **Kay, a landscape designer:** *For about a year now I have had a goal to publish articles about landscaping in some trade magazines. I've gone so far as writing articles that I think would be of interest to these publications. The bad news is that they are still sitting in my computer! I never seem to have the time to send them. The irony is that it would take far less effort to send them off than it took to write them, but I just don't get around to it. I am always so busy, I never have a moment to spare.*

What are some of your B items, both at work and at home? What action items would move you toward your goals, yet aren't time-sensitive? Smart people include at least one B item a day in their action planning. Once *you* adopt this habit, you'll find yourself moving forward faster—and with a greater sense of accomplishment.

C's Eat Away at Your Day

Have you ever had a really busy day at work only to get home and wonder, "What did I really accomplish today?" If so, your day was probably packed with C items. C items often involve mandatory or routine actions that have to get done—e.g., tax returns, bank deposits, routine reports, etc.—but don't move you toward your important goals in any substantial way. Whether they are or aren't time-sensitive is immaterial—we're prioritizing based upon value and satisfaction, not urgency. Resist marking items that are only time-sensitive as A's! Keep them as C's and do them if you need to, but don't fool yourself into thinking that a C that really, really, really needs to get done is an A.

Learn to Say No

Once you have set your priorities, having the time to pursue them involves learning how to say no to yourself and others. If activities are out of line with your goals and priorities, you need to learn to say no to them—sometimes even though they look fun, interesting, or worthwhile.

> **Frances, a dental office manager:** *I've often joked with my husband that when I die my headstone will read, "so many interests, so little time." I have a natural curiosity about things and I like to participate, so I am always getting overscheduled, overtired, and overwhelmed. I really need to think more carefully about what I say yes to.*

Smart people have learned how to say yes to the few important things and no to the many unimportant things. As simple as this seems, saying no can be a big deal. Here are a few handy phrases that will help you say no in an honest, straightforward, and respectful way:

THE TERRIFIC THREE: EVERYDAY PRACTICES FOR TIME MANAGEMENT EXCELLENCE

Daily to-do lists, master to-do lists, project planners, day planners, and calendar programs; whatever method or combination of methods works best for you, planning is key to using your time to its best advantage. Besides the obvious practice of writing down appointments, keeping a to-do list, and prioritizing tasks, the following daily practices will help keep your efforts on track:

1. Build in Flexibility

Even if you are the world's top time management guru, you will still get interrupted at work! The key is to build some flexibility into your schedule to allow for interruptions, distractions, and emergencies.

We suggest you avoid planning 100 percent of your day; leave at least a 30 percent margin for things that come up unexpectedly. To maintain a sense of completion when these interruptions occur, write them down, and check them off when done.

2. Fight the Tyranny of the Urgent

Urgent tasks are tempting because doing them gives us an immediate jolt of energy—another fire put out, another crisis averted! However, while urgent items may offer short-term benefits, their impact on your long-term goals is questionable. To cut down on your urgent items quota, we suggest not leaving things for the last minute. By using many of the skills taught in this book—such as assigning priorities, using a time-plan, and doing goal-oriented work during your peak performance times—you'll find yourself able to keep items that are important today from becoming urgent tomorrow.

3. Resist the Lure of the Trivial

How much of your valuable time and energy at work is taken up with trivial distractions that have no positive long-term impact on your life but do have a negative short-term effect on your productivity and sense of accomplishment? For example, gossiping with coworkers in the break room, surfing the Net for hot eBay buys, cleaning out your pencil cup, etc. While these are not bad activities in and of themselves, how much time are they eating up that you could be using in a more valuable way? Often we will turn to the trivial to avoid diving into the more significant (and more difficult) tasks before us. Someone once said, "If you face the hard things in life and do them, you will have an easy life. But if you only do the easy things in life, you will have a hard life." Smart people know that resisting trivial distractions and facing the more challenging tasks before them leads to a greater sense of accomplishment and satisfaction.

"I don't think I'm the right person for this job."

Sometimes we're asked to do something that is outside the scope of our experience, expertise, or skill level. We may say yes to this request either because we don't want to admit our limitations or we don't want to disappoint the person asking, but being honest up front saves panic down the road. It's always better to decline now rather than produce a mediocre result later on.

"I have a lot on my plate right now."

Other people don't know how much you have on your agenda at any given time, so letting them know that your dance card is full is one way to keep your action schedule manageable. However, resist the temptation to explain in great detail all your current projects: this can sound like whining and invite a discussion of how you could more efficiently work around the things you are already doing. Time, energy, and attention all have limits. Making others aware of your boundaries will prevent being overwhelmed and resentful in the future.

"I'm not comfortable with that."

From time to time a customer, coworker, or boss may ask you to do something you just don't feel right about. Whether it's an ethical or interpersonal issue, expressing your discomfort is a good way to negotiate your needs in a situation.

"I can't do it right now."

When you're willing to take something on but the timing is wrong, you can always say no for the moment but let the person know you would be happy to help at a later date. Make it clear that you will understand if they can't wait for you.

"I don't want to; No thank you, I'm not interested."

Direct? You bet. Sometimes it is necessary to just come out and say no! We have enough to do at work without saying yes to things we really don't want to do. Remember to say it *without* attitude but *with* respect.

"Doing this would require me to change" priorities.

This is a good phrase to use with a manager or client who wants you to do something that will cause a change in priorities—particularly if it's a change in priorities they have previously set. By letting them know the impact of taking on the new task, you are giving *them* the decision about which priorities should take precedence—which prevents *you* from being stuck between a rock and a hard place!

Summary

➤ It's important both to do things in the right way and to do the right things.

➤ Applying the 80/20 relationship can help you focus on the vital few things instead of the trivial many.

➤ The traditional ABC method of prioritizing is based on urgency.

➤ The ABC with a twist method is based on two factors: goal-relatedness and time-sensitivity.

A = Goal-related and time-sensitive

B = Goal-related but not time-sensitive

C = Not goal-related (may or may not be time-sensitive)

➤ Saying no helps create the time to pursue your highest priorities and goals.

CHAPTER 8

THE HABITS OF ACTION

In 1956, George Miller wrote a paper entitled "The Magical Number Seven, Plus or Minus Two." He had discovered that people can only focus on five to nine things at a time—anything beyond this has to be held in the unconscious mind. For most of us, it would be a dream come true if we only had to focus on five—or even nine—things! Unfortunately, in today's work environment we too often have to do too much in too little time, with too little energy and too little focus.

In 2004, a study by Kronos Incorporated of over a thousand workers found that 50 percent of those surveyed said they feel "overtired and overwhelmed" at work. A similar study in 2005 by the Families and Work Institute found that a full third of Americans are overworked; more than 50 percent of those surveyed said they are either handling too many tasks at the same time or are frequently interrupted during the workday—or both. In short, we are overloaded. Is it any wonder, then, that we have trouble getting jobs started, keeping them going, or finishing them up?

> **Suzanne, a financial advisor:** *My in-box has been piling up for weeks with items that would be good for business. I want to take some action on them but because none of*

them are really urgent I never get around to them. The pile is getting so high that things are beginning to fall off onto my desk! Every time I look at the stack I feel defeated, but I just don't know where to start.

Bob, a real estate broker: *We had a consultant come in six months ago to evaluate changes we should make in our physical space to increase efficiency and productivity. Most of the changes were small things: move a mirror, change the direction of a desk, rearrange the conference table, etc. I've done one or two of the things she recommended, but still haven't gotten around to most of the items. I feel guilty about this but it just seems like I never have the time.*

Frederick, an office manager: *We have an old copier in our office that's broken and would cost more money to repair than to replace. I called several charities to see if they wanted it but got no takers—but I don't want to pay the cost of having it hauled away. I've already bought a replacement, but the old machine is still sitting in my office. Every time I look at it I feel frustrated and think of the space it is taking up that could be better used.*

The people in all of the above examples knew what they wanted to accomplish and even what steps they had to take to get it done. However, at some point in the process—whether beginning, middle, or end—they had trouble taking the actions necessary to complete their objectives. Smart people understand that knowing what they want is only half the story—being able to take the actions necessary to accomplish it is the other. But it's not always easy: procrastination and feeling overwhelmed often keep us from being able to get where we want to go.

Over the past twenty years we've observed that smart people use three habits to get themselves to take action, even in tough times. These habits act as an inoculation against procrastination and feeling overwhelmed so that smart people are ultimately able to press through and get things done.

HABIT 1: CHUNKING DOWN: FOCUS ON THE TREES NOT THE FOREST

The secret of getting ahead is getting started. The secret of getting started is breaking your complex, overwhelming tasks into small, manageable tasks, and then starting on the first one. —Mark Twain

In the computer world, *chunking* means to break things into bits. To *chunk down* is to move from a whole to its parts; to *chunk up* is to move from parts to a whole, or from the specific to the general. A colleague gave us a simple example of different chunk sizes:

I was out to dinner with a friend and she ordered a gin martini. When it was my turn, I ordered a Bombay Sapphire martini, straight up, very cold, and with two olives. Clearly my comfort level when ordering a martini required a much smaller chunk size than my dining companion!

Chunking your projects and goals down into smaller pieces will help you take action more quickly and easily, while at the same time helping to combat the feeling of too much to do. The following case study examines how Jack and Sharon, first time authors, used chunking down to achieve their goal of publishing a book:

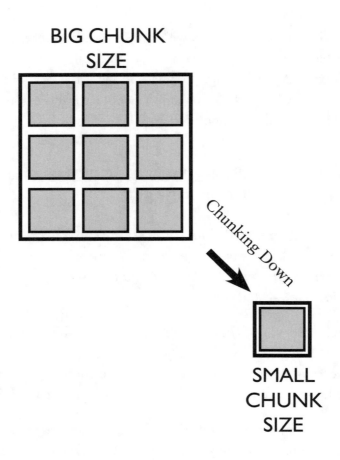

BIG CHUNK
SIZE

Chunking Down

SMALL
CHUNK
SIZE

CASE STUDY: Jack, Sharon, and Micro-Milestones

For several years, Jack and Sharon had wanted to write a book about their travel experiences in Italy. They had gotten as far as writing down some of the stories they wanted to include in the book. They took several classes on how to write travel books, but came out feeling even more confused than when they'd started. However, "One thing all the classes emphasized was to write a book proposal first," said Jack. "So we knew this would be a good place to start."

Traditional project management advises taking a large project—such as Jack and Sharon's plan to write a book—and breaking it down into predictable and logical milestones. In the case of publishing a book, these milestones might include:

Step 1: Write the book proposal.
Step 2: Submit the book proposal to a list of qualified agents.
Step 3: Follow up with agents.
Step 4: Sign with an agent.

The problem is that while these milestones may be logical and predictable, they may still be too large to handle—physically, mentally, or emotionally.

Jack and Sharon felt that the first step, writing the book proposal, was too much to take on; it just seemed overwhelming. Their solution was to break up this first step by chunking it down into eight smaller, more actionable micro-milestones. Their new plan looked like this:

Step 1: Write a two-page overview of the book.
Step 2: Write our one page author's biography.
Step 3: Research on Amazon to find similar books already in print.
Step 4: Write a comparison book write-up.
Step 5: Write a chapter-by-chapter outline.
Step 6: Write a sample chapter.
Step 7: Write a marketing plan.
Step 8: Put all the above together into polished book proposal form.

Jack and Sharon then set deadlines for each of these micro-milestones, and created a time-plan (see habit 3) that specified the dates and time periods when they would do their writing and research.

"Amazingly," says Sharon, "we completed all these steps for writing the book proposal within the set time frame and then took the same approach with the other milestones in the project, breaking them down into smaller actions. It took us six months of working like this, but we are now ready to find an agent and move on to getting our book published."

Mini-Tasks

Chunking down can also be applied to the smaller, everyday tasks on your to-do list. For example, an item that you keep transferring from day to day—or from week to week—may be a good candidate to bring to action by breaking into mini-tasks.

CASE STUDY: Steve and Mini-Tasks

Steve, a building contractor, had the item "put together bid for Sanborn Project" on his to-do list for three weeks, but had made little progress with it. He was procrastinating because the bid required additional research and was different from his usual proposals. Finally, in order to get it going, Steve changed "put together bid for Sanborn Project" into a series of smaller actions that he spread out over a week: on Monday, he worked on creating the project timeline; on Tuesday, he made calls to get pricing from a stone supplier; on Wednesday, he worked on labor costs, and so on. By the end of the week Steve had finished the bid and faxed it to the client.

By knowing to chunk items down as far as needed, the people in the above scenarios freed themselves to move into action. Whether you are breaking down a large project's milestones into micro-milestones, or transforming a stubborn item on your daily to-do list into mini-tasks, the key is to find the smaller chunks within the larger activity.

HABIT 2: TAKE ENERGETIC CREDIT FOR COMPLETION

When we have a big goal or task to work on, many of us wait—unnecessarily and sometimes to our detriment—until the entire project is finished before we experience any sense of accomplishment.

> **Ruth, a corporate planner:** *I've been working on producing an event that will take place in a few months. I've been consistently taking action from a to-do list I created for the event and everything that needs to be getting done is getting done. But I still feel overwhelmed by all the things that are left to do on the list. So even though technically I'm making progress, I don't feel any satisfaction.*

Often, even though we're achieving pieces of our projects and goals all the time, we don't fully acknowledge them. Smart people are in the habit of enthusiastically taking credit for any action they complete, no matter how seemingly small or insignificant. Smart people know not to wait until the big item is 100 percent done before experiencing closure. (Remember chapter 5: The Power of Closure? Closure generates energy.) Rather, smart people generate energy all along the way by recognizing each item they complete.

HABIT 3: TIME-PLANNING: PUT A STOP TO PUTTING IT OFF

According to research conducted by Timothy Pychyl at the University of Ottawa (2001), up to 70 percent of North Americans have a problem with procrastination. Some of the main causes of this procrastination include:

- Waiting to feel like the time—or our mood—is right to get things done

- Knowing what we want to accomplish, but not knowing how to go about it

- Feeling like the task itself is unpleasant, difficult, or overwhelming

- Having something more enjoyable and less difficult to do than the task at hand

Smart people are in the habit of using a time-plan to get beyond procrastination. A time-plan is a method of assigning blocks of time to those items you want to get done (but not a minute-by-minute description of your day!)

In *The Power of Full Engagement* (2003), Jim Loehr and Tony Schwartz describe several studies that demonstrated the power of determining when and where a specific action will occur. In one such study, between 75 and 100 percent of individuals who set a specific date and time to complete a task did so. By setting specific times and dates to work on an item, we put a structure in place that greatly increases the chances of completion.

THE 2 STEP TIME-PLAN

To harvest the power of planning and create your own time-plan, follow these two easy steps:

Step 1: Identify your power times for different types of activities.

Everyone has high and low periods of energy, attention, and focus. By knowing and understanding your own energy patterns you can create a time-plan that takes advantage of your personal rhythms. Reflect on your own energy patterns. When are your power times? Some questions that may help you:

> Do you like to plan for the next day, on the morning of the day or the night before?
>
> What is your most creative time during the day?
>
> Do you have an easier time doing difficult tasks earlier or later in the day?

Use your power times to take on your most difficult items. Use your downtime for more routine items and errands.

Step 2: Set aside blocks of time for getting certain things done.

Keeping in mind your power times, go through your calendar and schedule a specific day and period of time when you will work on an item. Time periods ranging from fifteen minutes to two hours are most effective. Avoid the temptation of trying to get everything done in one marathon sitting. Remember when you were a student and you'd put off studying for the big test until the night before, then stay up all night cramming? It wasn't a good strategy, was it? You'll yield better results if you break the project down—say, into five one-hour time slots—over a few days. Every hour or so, schedule a ten-minute break from your task; this will both keep your brain from getting tired and give it a chance to process any information, so that you can return to your project refreshed.

Lastly, don't just plan your time in your head—write it down! Whether you use a PDA, a calendar contact program, or a plain old date book, keeping a written record of your time-plan is key.

Summary

➤ People can only focus on five to nine things at a time; anything beyond this has to be held in the unconscious mind.

➤ Procrastination and feeling overwhelmed are the two biggest obstacles to taking action.

➤ Smart people have developed three specific habits to help themselves overcome procrastination and over-whelm and take action:

  › Habit 1: Chunking Down. Break projects into micro-milestones and to-do items into mini-tasks.

  › Habit 2: Taking Credit for Completion. Acknowledge your progress all along the way by recognizing and generating energy from the completion of any micro-milestones or mini-tasks.

  › Habit 3: Time-Planning. Overcome procrastination and facilitate action by understanding your power times and dedicating specific blocks of time to projects/tasks.

PART 3

CONFLICT: SMART PEOPLE DANCE WITH FIRE

Conflict is inevitable, but combat is optional.

—Max Lucade

CHAPTER 9

BUILDING RAPPORT WITH ALMOST ANYONE

Think of a time when you really connected with another person, when you felt effortlessly heard and understood. That feeling was *natural rapport*. Rapport leads to better communication, improved collaboration, and more productive relationships.

Unfortunately, we don't have natural rapport with everyone! However, since we have to work with all sorts, when rapport doesn't come naturally, smart people create it.

SOCIAL RAPPORT

In those cases where natural rapport doesn't exist, *social rapport* can help you build a bridge between you and another person. It's a critical skill for job interviews, client interactions, coaching, sales, and team building. In all of these situations we can unwittingly undermine our objectives by distancing ourselves from those who talk, think, or behave differently than we do. Social rapport presumes that when others see in us behaviors that remind them of themselves, they become more trusting and open to our ideas; it's achieved by respectfully matching the other person's body language and conversational style.

Building rapport requires focusing on the other person and observing how they use their voice, body, and words to communicate. If you're too busy focusing on your own concerns, worries, and fears, your attention will be drawn inward—away from the other person. Instead, mentally push distracting thoughts to the back burner and focus your attention on the person in front of you (or on the other end of the phone).

Mirroring

A key technique for building social rapport is mirroring. The three principal areas for mirroring are body language, tone of voice, and words.

Reflect Their Body Language

We recommend starting the mirroring process with the other person's body language. Assess the person's posture and bearing, then try to mirror your observations with your own body—subtly and respectfully! For example, if a person is sitting forward in their chair attentively, you could mirror this by sitting up and looking alert.

CASE STUDY: Ursula and the Job Interview

Ursula is an operations supervisor for a paper product manufacturer. She has applied for a job transfer to another department within the same company and is about to be interviewed by Dorothy, one of the firm's HR team. Ursula is really excited about the career advancement this new job offers, so it's important to her to make a good impression and create rapport.

After smiling and saying hello, Ursula quickly assesses Dorothy's body language. She notices that Dorothy is leaning back in her chair and looks relaxed; Dorothy makes frequent eye contact, but also looks away from time to time; she gestures only very minimally with her arms and hands.

Ursula begins to mirror Dorothy's body language: she moves from her bolt upright, edge-of-the-seat position to a more relaxed posture. She scoots back in her chair, becomes a little less rigid. Also, because Dorothy isn't maintaining continual eye contact, Ursula, too, looks away from time to time—although under normal circumstances Ursula's natural behavior is to lock onto a person's eyes and not let go. Furthermore, because Dorothy tends to keep her own hands quietly resting on her desk, Ursula resists the urge to use the bold, sweeping arm gestures she is famous for.

Reflect Their Tone of Voice

Tone of voice consists primarily of volume, speed, and inflection. Strong emotions, such as anger, are often expressed in a loud voice—this is one situation where mirroring should not be used! Shouting back at someone will do little to smooth the waters and create rapport. Instead, in situations of hot tempers and strident language, stay calm and bring the other person down to your level—don't escalate to theirs.

Several factors influence the rate at which people speak, including geography (think New Yorkers versus Texans), level of excitement, and feelings of urgency. For example, Ursula naturally speaks quite quickly, while Dorothy speaks in a slower and more monotone voice. In order to mirror Dorothy, Ursula deliberately slows down her speech.

Reflect Their Words

Often, if you're paying close attention you'll notice that people have favorite words they regularly weave into their sentences. Social rapport can be greatly enhanced if you use these same words (although you must be careful not to mimic). For example, after Ursula notices that Dorothy has used the word "synergy" several times within the first few minutes of the conversation—and even though this isn't a popular word in her own vocabulary —Ursula then makes a point of using "synergy" herself when the opportunity arises.

Getting in Step with Working Styles

Our *working style* is the primary way we approach and deal with people and situations at work. If you understand the way you like to work, it becomes easier to create rapport with others whose working style may be different than yours. Each of the four working styles reviewed below reflects two specific qualities: *emotional expressiveness* and *assertiveness*.

Emotional Expressiveness. Your personal level of emotional expressiveness is a function of how much you show or hold back your emotions. Do you use colorful language in your conversations? (Higher) Or are you more understated? (Lower) Are you a fast talker, or do you speak at a slow and easy pace? Is there a lot of intensity and excitement in your voice, or do you usually sound calm and relaxed? Do you talk with your hands, or do you hold them by your side when speaking?

Assertiveness.   Your personal level of assertiveness is a function of how much or how little you try to influence and control the actions and opinions of those around you. When working in a group, do you end up being the leader? (Higher) Or do you usually find yourself one of the team? (Lower) Do you get impatient when people take too long to get their point across, or do you wait patiently for them to finish? Are you forceful and direct in your opinion, or more reserved about expressing what you think?

Working Styles

Analytical.   People with an analytical working style have a low degree of assertiveness and a low degree of emotional expressiveness. People with this style tend to focus more on the facts of situations than any feelings they or others may have; they tend to evaluate situations objectively and gather lots of data before making any decisions. Words that describe the analytical style include serious, organized, logical, reserved, and factual.

Not surprisingly, people with this style are good problem solvers and fact finders. They are patient, can work well on their own, and often excel in areas of finance, science, and technology. Those with an analytical working style are often uncomfortable expressing feelings and have been known to avoid making a difficult decision by overanalyzing.

Some ways you could mirror someone with an analytical working style include engaging in only minimal facial expressions and vocal inflections, using precise and specific language, and focusing on the details of a project.

Driver.   People with a driver working style have a high degree of assertiveness and a low degree of emotional expressiveness. People with this style know where they want to go and how they are going to get there; they are good at managing tasks and are results-oriented. Words that describe the driver style include independent, decisive, intense, efficient, and competitive.

Drivers are often high achievers who can take charge of a situation and make quick decisions; drivers are focused on their goals and aren't afraid to take the risks needed to accomplish them. People with a driver working style are often lawyers, surgeons, and CEOs. Drivers can sometimes work so quickly that they overlook important details and make mistakes. (Not so good if you're a surgeon—or their patient!)

Some ways you could mirror someone with a driver style include making direct eye contact, moving quickly, speaking forcefully and rapidly, and getting right down to the bottom line.

Amiable.   People with an amiable working style have a low degree of assertiveness and a high degree of emotional expressiveness. People with this style are usually cooperative, friendly, supportive, patient, and relaxed. Their sensitivity to the feelings of others makes them good team players and well suited to the helping professions. They are often nurses, therapists, and teachers. However, they can be less than effective when they have to make a quick decision, or deal with conflict.

Some ways you could mirror someone with an amiable style include displaying a friendly facial expression, making frequent eye contact, utilizing nonaggressive gestures and body language, and asking them how they feel about things.

Expressive.   People with an expressive working style have a high degree of assertiveness and a high degree of emotional expressiveness. People with this style are outgoing, persuasive, enthusiastic, friendly, and sociable; they are able to motivate and generate excitement in others, and are well suited to high profile positions that require them to make public presentations; thus those of this style are often found as trainers, actors, salespeople, and so on.

When someone with an expressive working style is upset, they often communicate their feelings with a lot of intensity; if criticized, they may lash out with a verbal attack. People with an expressive style can seem overwhelming to less assertive styles because when they are enthusiastic about an idea they press for quick action and may overlook important details.

Some ways you could mirror someone with an expressive working style include using rapid hand and arm gestures, speaking quickly with lots of animation and inflection, and using language that is exciting and persuasive.

Returning to the case study above: Ursula has an expressive style but she quickly realizes that Dorothy has an analytical style. To mirror Dorothy, Ursula reduces her arm movements, minimizes her facial expressions, and answers Dorothy's questions in detail, conversing in small, logical steps rather than the big excited leaps that are her natural style.

Pacing and Leading

Pacing is a powerful, active listening skill that complements mirroring. Pacing requires being open to what the other person is saying and following their lead. When pacing, listening is your primary concern, talking is secondary. Pacing someone who is upset and angry would mean listening to *whatever* they say without getting defensive or responding. Pacing someone who is sad would mean showing compassion, listening to what they say and offering small reassurances without offering ways that they might feel better. Smart people begin most critical conversations by pacing. They listen not only to the words they are hearing but also try to get in step with the working style of the other person. Listening actively but silently (except for the occasional nod or "uh-huh" of understanding) gives people room to express themselves.

People want to be heard. As Norman Fischer says in *Taking Our Places* (2004):

> Being heard does feel great. We all want to be listened to—we all need it. Many of us suffer terribly for lack of it ... The practice of listening will always raise more questions than it answers. In this it is fertile soil for the development of true human maturity.

The more people feel that you are listening to them, the more they will be able to listen to you when it is your turn to speak. In most conversations, there's a natural point at which pacing shifts into leading. You begin leading by:

- Asking a question
- Offering to help
- Gathering information
- Making a promise
- Expressing an opinion
- Disagreeing

The opportunity to lead may come when there is a lull in the conversation, when you sense that the other person wants you to say something, or when you are asked a question.

For example, back in our case study, Ursula begins pacing Dorothy. Dorothy spends the first five minutes of the interview describing the open position and what kind of skills it requires. She emphasizes the need for synergy with the existing team and the qualities the department head is looking for. Ursula stays quiet and allows Dorothy to speak uninterrupted, with an occasional nod or "uh-huh" to show that she is following.

Dorothy says, "I've read your application but would appreciate it if you could tell me, in your own words, why you want this position and what you will bring to it."

Still mirroring Dorothy, Ursula now starts to lead the conversation: Ursula explains comprehensively and confidently what she will bring to the new job if she gets it.

Leading, as the name suggests, means that you speak and move the conversation forward. Only one person can be leading —and one person pacing—at a time. If both people are leading, then nobody is listening (sound familiar?). And if both people are pacing, then nothing is happening! There are no hard and fast rules about when to lead and when to pace, but it may help to think of conversation as a dance: when dancing, you want to pay close attention to your partner and move according to his or her cues.

NATURAL RAPPORT

Natural rapport, unlike social rapport, is the deep, heartfelt connection you have with certain people you know. This type of rapport develops naturally over time and isn't dependent on applied techniques. However, there are times when natural rapport between two people can feel diminished or blocked, when the usual affinity is replaced by awkwardness and the normal easy flow of the relationship becomes stilted and artificial.

Smart people understand that natural rapport only happens when they (and the other person) are being true to their own values, feelings, and thoughts. Whenever your boundaries are overstepped and you feel hurt by someone you feel close to (or excluded, disrespected, diminished, or manipulated), you most likely will distance yourself from that person. However, if you don't talk to the other person about your feelings—because you are afraid of their reaction,

CHANGING INTERESTS

At times, the natural rapport you share with another person may happen simply because you're both involved in a similar interest or experience. Once that interest disappears, the degree of natural rapport may decrease, or even disappear entirely.

For example, working on a long-term project with colleagues, sharing challenges and triumphs along the way, can create strong bonds of friendship. You may then enjoy a strong feeling of mutual understanding and rapport—seemingly independent of the original project. But then the project ends. Slowly the rapport erodes. Conversations become less frequent and more forced.

This may seem depressing, but it's also natural. When authentic rapport ends like this, try to think of it as a passing gift.

or you think that they might think that you are making a mountain out of a molehill—then the distancing process will only continue. Then, although you may still have a close friendship, the satisfaction that comes from deep, natural rapport will be missing.

Sometimes this situation is reversed, and *we* are the ones who have overstepped another's boundaries! We may have broken a promise and never acknowledged it, said something hurtful and never apologized, or bent the truth to get what we want. Regardless, left unresolved, hurt feelings will dilute natural rapport.

As with many things, communication is the answer. As soon as you talk with the other person about what's been going on, the air will clear and you'll feel close again—maybe even closer. (Our reasons for not speaking up are usually ways for us to avoid an uncomfortable conversation. See chapter 13 for techniques on how to speak up and be heard.)

Summary

▶ Rapport improves communication, facilitates collaboration, and makes for more productive relationships and
conversations.

▶ There are two types of rapport: natural and social.

▶ Natural rapport is the deep connection you feel with
people who make you feel heard and understood
effortlessly; natural rapport isn't dependent on specific
techniques.

▶ Social rapport can help you build a bridge between
yourself and another person; social rapport is achieved
by respectfully matching the other person's body language and conversational style.

▶ Mirroring is a technique for building social rapport. It
involves subtly and respectfully reflecting another person's body language, tone of voice, and words.

    › The key areas for reflecting body language are
eye contact, body posture, and facial expression.

    › The key areas for reflecting voice tone are vol-
ume, speed, and inflection.

    › When reflecting words, be aware of the other
person's vocabulary and repeat back words that
they use often.

▶ Knowing a person's working style—analytical, driver,
amiable, or expressive—helps you to adjust your style
to match theirs.

▶ People love to be heard; the more they feel heard the
more they'll be able to listen to you.

➤ Pacing improves your critical listening skills. When in doubt, always begin a conversation by pacing; when the moment presents itself—usually as a question to you or a lull in the conversation—then begin leading.

➤ Natural rapport is diminished if you (or the other person) stop being true to your own values and feelings. By talking about what's really going on, rapport can be renewed and even improved.

➤ Natural rapport can be the function of a shared project or interest. Sometimes when the mutual interest disappears so does the rapport.

CHAPTER 10

FACING TENSE TIMES

There are times at work when we find ourselves on the receiving end of someone else's strong emotions—an irate customer, a venting coworker, an angry supervisor, a frustrated vendor, etc. In each of these situations, the other person is behaving in a way that may get our guard up and influence the way we respond.

For example, imagine an angry customer calls you and yells, "You people messed up my order again! I can't believe you can't get it together over there!" Your first reaction may be to say, "Hey, *I* can't believe I have to deal with morons like you who don't even know how to act in a civil way!" However, being the seasoned professional you are, you probably know that if you actually said this (rather than just thinking it) you would quickly find yourself in a dark downward spiral where nobody wins and nothing gets resolved.

Smart people understand that you cannot stop other people from venting their feelings—even when this venting is ineffective, immature, or irresponsible. So instead of fruitlessly trying to change the behavior of others, smart people look at how they can manage their own internal responses and reactions. While you can't fully disengage your fight-or-flight mechanism, you can put together a toolbox of practical skills that will help you deal with even the most annoying of people in a way that reduces your own stress level and defuses combustible situations.

SKILL 1: CHOOSE YOUR INTERPRETATION

A great deal of the stress we experience is tied to our perception of an event rather than the event itself.

CASE STUDY: Greg and the Message from His Boss

It's the end of the week and Greg, a financial analyst at a large real estate investment company, is preparing to go home. One last glance at his email in-box shows that he has a new message from his boss, Maggie. He reads, "I need to talk to you about the reports you gave me." Greg is caught off-guard. Immediately he starts to wonder what he might have done wrong. "Is there a glaring inaccuracy? Did she receive a complaint from an investor?" As Greg takes the elevator to Maggie's office he nervously broods over one bad scenario after another.

When Greg arrives at Maggie's office, her assistant explains that Maggie has just left for a weekend in the mountains with her family and won't be reachable until Monday. Breaking into a cold sweat, Greg tries her cell phone several times as he drives home but gets no answer. Greg spends the entire weekend preparing his defense—he's been under a lot of pressure, he's got a good track record, etc.—he's not going to lay down and be criticized!

At long last, Monday rolls around. Greg strides into Maggie's office, mentally prepared to deflect any criticism. He says to Maggie, "You wanted to see me about the reports?" Maggie smiles, "Yes. I looked at those reports you prepared and I couldn't believe what a thorough job you did given the short amount of time you had to pull them together. I just wanted to really thank you. Good work!"

Outside Maggie's door, Greg collapses in a puddle of relief (internally, at least!). All of that stress for nothing! While Greg's reaction was real, the cause he imagined was not. By automatically choosing a negative interpretation of Maggie's email, Greg created stress where there didn't need to be any. He focused on how he was going to fight back and protect himself instead of just admitting that he didn't know what this was about and would have to wait until Monday to find out. Also, although this did not turn out to be the difficult situation he imagined, if Maggie really had been angry with him, Greg's negative mental stance would have added extra, unneeded fuel to a heated situation.

Every situation—especially difficult ones—has more than one interpretation. If we do as smart people do, we'll choose an interpretation that helps resolve the situation rather than exacerbate it. This act of consciously changing interpretations is often referred to as *reframing*.

REFRAMING PRACTICE

Read each of the following scenarios and come up with one negative and one positive interpretation for each. (We've answered the first one as an example.)

1. A customer calls complaining about a late delivery.

Negative interpretation: *Some people have nothing better to do than complain.*

Positive interpretation: *Maybe our delivery system could use some upgrading.*

2. Your office manager is upset about the escalating cost of printing supplies.

Negative interpretation:

Positive interpretation:

3. An upset customer calls about a repair not covered by the warranty.

Negative interpretation:

Positive interpretation:

4. A salesperson has promised the customer something that you cannot deliver.

Negative interpretation:

Positive interpretation:

SKILL 2: STOP THE SPIRAL!

Unfortunately, most of us have been involved in conversations that have spiraled hopelessly out of control. The following case study will help you understand how to avoid the upsetting and unproductive cycle of spiraling out of control.

CASE STUDY: Val and Veronica

Val, an insurance broker, works in a small office with five other people. Recently she has been getting more and more annoyed with Veronica, the new agent who sits in the cubicle behind hers. Veronica has strong opinions about *everything* and Val can't stand the way Veronica spouts off about things she knows nothing about. This morning, Veronica is busy broadcasting her opinions about dieting and health: "All this talk about obesity and fast foods is just hype! I eat plenty of fast food and I'm okay!"

Val has a mild heart condition and has spent the last four years closely monitoring her diet and learning about nutrition, so Veronica's uninformed remarks really tick her off. However, she bites her tongue and says nothing—until Veronica says, "How can it be harmful to eat fat? Our body is made up of fat!"

Then, before she can stop herself, Val calls over the cubicle wall, "Can you keep your voice down? I'm trying to concentrate!" Veronica takes offense at Val's annoyed tone and shoots back, "What's wrong with you? Did you get up on the wrong side of the bed this morning or something?" Without thinking, Val responds, "No! I just need a break from your talking!"

The conversation is now spiraling out of control. Veronica comes back at Val with an even more disrespectful reply and Val responds with more of the same. Each round of insults is worse than the one before, with voices getting louder and tempers hotter.

Let's look at how this conflict trap could have been avoided. Instead of adding fuel to the fire, Val could have de-escalated the situation by doing any of the following

Apologizing

As soon as Val realized that her remark conveyed a tone of annoyance that provoked Veronica, she could have apologized by saying something like, "I'm sorry, I'm a bit on edge today."

Interrupting

The spiral could have been interrupted by Val choosing not to respond to Veronica's "wrong side of the bed" comment. Remember: it's never too late to hold your tongue and stay quiet. A moment of silence can give you the time you need to stop yourself from automatically zinging back yet another negative response.

LEARN, DON'T BLAME

In every difficult situation you can choose whether to blame or to learn. If you choose to blame, the situation is unlikely to get resolved—because you'll always be talking to the other person from a negative point of view. On the other hand, if you choose to learn from the interaction, you'll be reacting and listening from a more compassionate point of view—and the situation is that much more likely to get resolved.

Think of a difficult situation that you have recently been involved in. Did you approach this situation more from the perspective of assigning blame or of learning?

Rephrasing

Val could have rephrased her comment as soon as she real-ized that it sounded offensive. She could have said something like, "What I mean is, I'm having a hard time understanding the pre-mium structure on this policy and I'd appreciate a bit of quiet."

SKILL 3: CLEAN UP THE PUT-DOWN

Often said in a sarcastic or joking tone, put-downs carry a wallop when they are delivered, even though the words themselves can seem harmless enough. This situation can be a tough one to deal with because the real issue is usually hidden. The nasty edge of put-downs is often due to resentment—the distillation of an anger that isn't directly expressed.

CASE STUDY: Katrina and Jonathan

Katrina and Jonathan are buyers for a nationwide furni-ture store. They work out of the same office but see each other there only one week every month when they get a break from their heavy travel schedules. They've always gotten along, but recently Jonathan has seemed upset about something and been difficult to deal with. This particular afternoon, Katrina is reviewing a new inventory list from one of her suppliers. When Jonathan passes by her desk, he says in a sarcastic tone of voice, "Boy, Katrina, I wish *I* had time to just sit and read all day long." Katrina is taken aback. She looks up to say something, but Jonathan is already halfway across the office.

The next day, Katrina approaches Jonathan during a break and says, "You seemed really stressed yesterday." Jonathan replies, "Of course I'm stressed! I'm twice as busy as you and I have nobody to help me. I'm on the road three weeks a month and when I'm here I don't even have enough time to catch up!"

Katrina responds, "You know, I have just as much work as you—maybe even more—and I travel the same amount of time you do." Jonathan just sighs and shakes his head, then walks away. Katrina is left confused—what the heck just happened?

In this scenario, Katrina is unaware that Jonathan's real problem lies below the surface. Put-downs—such as Jonathan's "wish *I* had time to read" comment—are unpleasant smoke screens that conceal key issues. By naturally reacting to and defending herself against Jonathan's insults, Katrina is unwittingly dealing with the smoke rather than the fire itself. Her sincere desire to resolve this difficult situation means that she will have to discover what is really bothering Jonathan. To this end, instead of cornering him in the coffee room and firing a direct question, Katrina would have been better off using the following three techniques:

1. Ask a Few Questions to Start a Genuine Dialogue

Dialogues are best started with questions rather than statements (or worse still, accusations!). Beginning a conversation by asking, "You seem a little upset today, is everything okay?" offers an opportunity for the other person to respond openly, whereas a statement such as, "You're in a rotten mood today!" will likely evoke a defensive response that won't foster genuine dialogue.

2. Listen Without Defending or Arguing

Even if what the other person says sounds unreasonable or untrue, try to honor their point of view by listening as much as possible without judgment (see Switch Filters in chapter 11). Try to hear the message *underneath* what is being said.

3. Get to the Real Issue

While it's not healthy to assume that every put-down is the result of something you unwittingly did or didn't do, we've found that resentment can often be short-circuited by asking a question like, "I don't know what I've done to upset you but I want to resolve it. I can only fix it if you let me know what's bothering you."

SKILL 4: DIG INTO SMOOTHING

Smoothing is a strategy some people use to avoid conflict. When we smooth, we pretend that everything is okay, at least on the surface, when in reality, the situation is a conflict waiting to erupt—and it will bubble to the surface like hot lava when we least expect it.

CASE STUDY: Jose and Rob

Jose is Rob's supervisor at a heating and ventilating company. Due to a surge in business, Rob has been getting further and further behind on restocking the sheet metal inventory. Rob is a smoother—when Jose calls him to ask about inventory status, Rob tells him everything's fine.

Ten days later, Jose is contacted by an upset foreman who is missing several key components. Jose calls Rob and asks what's going on. Rob says, "A minor mishap, everything's under control." Jose, not fully satisfied this time, asks, "Are you sure? This is a big job and we can't afford a delay." "I'm on top of it," Rob assures him. "Leave it to me."

Needless to say, the situation gets worse instead of better. The next time Jose calls Rob he's upset: "Rob, what the heck's going on over there? I've got three sites yelling at me for materials that were never delivered! How come you keep telling me everything's okay when the inventory's obviously totally messed up?" Anger rises from the pit of Rob's stomach and the words burst out of Rob: "I've only got one pair of hands! The system I use is outdated and slow and you guys expect miracles! I'm sick of everyone blaming me for everything!"

No matter how Jose and Rob resolve the situation, the costs in time, money, and morale are already greater than they needed to be. Because Jose believed Rob's smoothing tactics, he didn't check on the real state of affairs with inventory earlier. Now, with Rob backed into a corner, Jose's job is much harder than if he had responded differently earlier in the situation.

Here are three techniques Jose could have used to avoid this difficult situation:

1. Ask a Probing Question

Don't tolerate vagueness—and don't be put off by the discomfort that you may feel when checking the validity of an answer. By posing specific, detailed questions, you'll help avoid problems down the road.

2. Avoid Accusations

Use a nonaccusing tone by keeping your voice soft, and avoid language that makes it sound as if you are accusing the other person. Remember: if a person is holding something back, they're probably doing so because they want to avoid conflict—not because they are dishonest.

3. Don't Overreact

By following the two steps above you'll probably uncover some hidden issue that wasn't being dealt with. Don't overreact. Assuming that the other person hasn't done something really terrible, most problems can be resolved simply by open communication.

SKILL 5: APPRECIATE OPINIONS FOR WHAT THEY ARE: OPINIONS

According to the Encarta dictionary, an opinion is "the view somebody takes about a certain issue, especially when it is based solely on personal judgment." Just because we agree with another person's opinion doesn't mean that it's right—it just means we hold the same opinion. Similarly, just because we disagree with someone's opinion doesn't mean it's wrong—it's just different than ours.

Differing opinions are at the heart of many difficult conversations. The illogical logic is: because my opinion differs from yours—and my opinion is right—I have to try to prove that you are wrong and I am right. It's this last part where we get into mischief. For some reason, when we encounter a differing opinion, we feel compelled to try to change the other person's mind—as if our opinion is less valid because they don't agree!

Try this simple exercise:

Write down one thing that you really like but a friend of yours doesn't. For example: musical comedy, sushi, basketball, scary movies, flipping channels, short hair, olives, windy days, flossing, sitcoms, dancing, hiking, driving fast, etc.

Now imagine trying to convince your friend that he or she really does like one of these things—say, olives. Imagine describing the wonderful taste of olives, their beautiful shape, glossy skins, etc. Would your passionate description of the magnificence of the olive change your friend's opinion about them? Probably not.

Try another tactic: subtly tell them that they are wrong not to like olives. Is your friend's opinion now changed? Probably not. Next, point out all of the logical reasons to like olives—e.g., olives are high in nutrients, essential fatty acids, etc. Has the opinion changed? Still, probably not. Maybe if you levitated and said it was a direct side effect of olive eating, *then* your friend would change his or her opinion about olives! Then again, maybe not.

The point is that when we have strong opinions about something, we don't easily change them—and certainly not just because somebody tells us that we should, no matter how compelling the reasons. Smart people listen to what others have to say and are comfortable considering opinions different than their own. They can have two or more opinions on the table at the same time without feeling pressured to change them or relinquish their own. If I like olives and you don't, that's fine. You have your opinion and I have mine. Both are valid and both can exist without conflict.

By not narrowly focusing on whether we agree or disagree with another person's opinion, our attention can be directed toward really hearing what he or she has to say.

SKILL 6: SAY I, NOT YOU

Smart people make it a habit when they are upset or angry to use the word "I" rather than "you." By using "I" you are conveying to the other person that you are making a statement about how *you* feel. "I messages" decrease the tendency toward defensive non-listening—and *increase* the odds that the other person will actually hear what you have to say. "You" is more accusatory and can give the impression of blame. For example, which of the following makes you feel more defensive: "When you promise you'll take care of the paperwork and you don't, I feel frustrated." Or, "You never do what you say you're going to do. You're really frustrating to work with."

One quick way to know if you are expressing a feeling or an opinion—or a thought disguised as a feeling—is to use the 'think' substitution test. For example, imagine you want to say something like: "I feel you are being a real jerk when you don't replace the ink cartridge in the printer." Now substitute "think" for "feel": "I think you are being a real jerk when you don't replace the ink cartridge in the printer." In this case "think" and "feel" are interchangeable—which means what you are expressing is a thought, not a feeling.

On the other hand, when you cannot substitute one word for the other, you are conveying a real feeling, as in, "I feel uneasy whenever you tell me there's nothing to worry about." The sentence "I think uneasy whenever you tell me there's nothing to worry about" doesn't make any sense—you are expressing a feeling.

Summary

► Smart people don't try to stop others from venting their feelings; instead, they mangse their own reactions by having a toolbox of useful skills that you can use, too.

► Skill 1: Choose Your Interpretation. Choose how you interpret difficult situations; don't automatically assume the worst or dwell on the negative.

► Skill 2: Stop the Spiral! Don't fall into the trap of returning hostile fire and letting angry conversations spiral out of control.

► Skill 3: Clean Up the Put-Downs. Clean up put-downs by being willing to look for the real—usually hidden—cause of another person's resentful comments.

► Skill 4: Dig into Smoothing. Ask probing questions; getting to the bottom of an issue now is far better than having it erupt uncontrollably later.

► Skill 5: Appreciate Opinions for What They Are: Opinions. Realize that you don't have to change or discredit the opinions of others just because they differ from yours.

► Skill 6: Say I, Not You. Using "you" can easily sound accusatory; by using "I" instead, your statements about your feelings and opinions are more likely to actually be heard.

CHAPTER 11

GETTING TO KNOW YOUR NEGATIVE FILTERS

Natural scientists believe that biodiversity helps ensure the survival of an ecosystem: animals and plants learn to adapt to each other. Similarly, many of our projects at work require us to collaborate with different types of people. Smart people know that a diversity of talents, points of view, and styles can bring a magical element to the team effort, creating a whole far greater than the sum of its parts.

A FLEETING NEGATIVE THOUGHT

Often, however, we greet diversity at work with a clenched jaw. Many collaborative efforts have failed because people reacted negatively to one another. When an initial negative reaction turns into a more entrenched negative filter, a huge problem can develop. For example, think about someone you know whom you consider difficult to work with. What are some of the negative names you call them? (Not necessarily aloud or to other people!) "Jerk," "loser," and "stupid" are on most people's top ten lists.

If these negative thoughts about others are merely fleeting judgments that you quickly release, they won't seriously impact your relationship. For example, if your boss gets grumpy at an early morning meeting, you may immediately think, "He's such a jerk!" However, if by noon you're over it and back to thinking that your boss is a pretty decent person, then the "jerk" judgment was just a temporary and circumstantial negative opinion.

A PERSISTENT NEGATIVE POINT OF VIEW

However, if you have a persistent negative point of view about another person (Bob in accounting?) or a group of persons (your customers?)—a negative point of view that sticks in your head and you're continually gathering more evidence to justify—then you're in the process of developing a negative filter. This will have a detrimental effect on your relationship with that person or group of people.

For example, let's say that after your boss got grumpy at the early morning meeting you found yourself thinking, "He's such a jerk—he always is!" And then by noon, you're even more annoyed. You complain about him to a colleague, "He was his usual jerky self yet again!" Meanwhile, frustration churns inside as you think, "I *hate* working for this jerk." At this point, you're trapped in a negative filter.

When you view someone through a negative filter it's as if a screen comes between you and the other person: whatever the person says or does is distorted by this screen—and becomes the evidence that proves the validity of the negative filter. Conversely, whatever you say to them goes through the same screen, and often develops a negative edge in the process, usually conveyed—subtly or otherwise—by your tone of voice and facial expression.

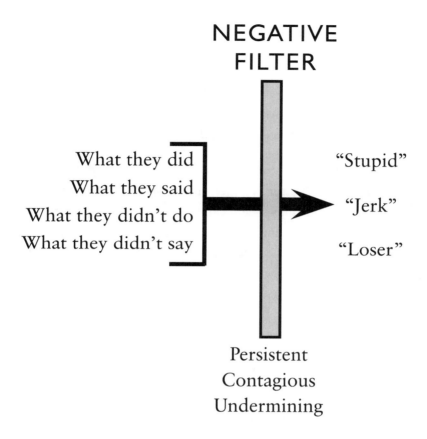

NEGATIVE FILTER

What they did
What they said
What they didn't do
What they didn't say

"Stupid"

"Jerk"

"Loser"

Persistent
Contagious
Undermining

CASE STUDY: Negative Filter on Flight 22

We saw a clear example of negative filters in action during a flight between New York and San Francisco. At one point during the flight, a nearby passenger asked the flight attendant for a cup of coffee. She happily obliged. However, as he picked up the cup of coffee, he accidentally spilled it on himself. The flight attendant hurried back over to him with a towel and helped him clean up the mess. She then sympathetically asked if she could bring him another cup. He said yes and she returned with the fresh coffee. Guess what? He accidentally spilled his coffee again! This time the flight attendant reacted very differently. She looked disapprovingly at the mess, and, in the tone of a parent talking to a 4-year-old, said, "We have to be more careful now, don't we?" At this, the passenger—who minutes before had appeared mature and professional—seemed to regress and begin acting as if he were a 4-year-old!

The moral of the story is that you are allowed to make a mistake once, but if you make the same mistake a second time the people around you may see your behavior as a pattern and develop negative filters about you as a result. In this case, for the flight attendant, after the passenger spilled his coffee a second time, a negative "klutz" filter replaced her original sympathetic filter and then—as observed by both us and the passenger—her tone of voice, body language, and words all perfectly aligned themselves to this new negative point of view.

Negative Filters Are Contagious

If this sounds horrible, that's because it is! Negative filters are one of the most common causes of conflict in the workplace (both among coworkers and between staff and customers), and sadly, we often pass our negative filters on. Here's how it works: Imagine you're on a coffee break with some of your longtime colleagues and Joe, the new guy who has just joined the department. When the subject happens to turn to Sally in sales, you jokingly mention that she's really pushy. A few others enthusiastically agree. As a result, Joe has now unwittingly taken on a negative "pushy" filter about Sally, courtesy of the coffee break group. Needless to say, when Joe finally meets Sally, the negative filter already in his head will cause him to quietly gather evidence of her "pushy" nature and the perception may become entrenched.

Negative Filters Undermine Collaboration

At this point, you're probably saying, "Okay—but sometimes they really *are* jerks. Sometimes they really *are* pushy." It's human nature to have negative thoughts about other people and it's pointless pretending that we don't. The point is not to focus on them. If you focus your attention on these negative opinions/filters you'll get sucked into a downward spiral and be unable to collaborate with the other person. After all, if you have a negative filter about them they'll almost certainly develop a negative filter about you! People are very sensitive: no matter how subtle the behavior, others tend to know when they are being judged through a negative filter.

In addition to this blow to healthy collaboration, negative filters also increase your stress and lower your satisfaction level. Projects always take longer to accomplish when you work with adversaries instead of allies.

CASE STUDY: Yvonne and the Skeptical Patient

Yvonne is a nurse practitioner at a busy family doctor's office. When a routine medical checkup revealed that Gabe, one of her patients, had higher than average cholesterol, Yvonne called him to set up an appointment to talk about ways he might reduce his cholesterol and risk of heart disease. After making the appointment, Yvonne said to the front desk manager, "This should be interesting. In the past he's always questioned the efficacy of every treatment I've suggested." Without realizing it, Yvonne was already viewing Gabe through a negative "argumentative" filter.

The day of Gabe's appointment arrived. After having his blood pressure checked, Gabe sat down to talk with Yvonne. Yvonne looked over his blood test results and began to outline ways Gabe could reduce his saturated fat intake and increase his exercise. In response, Gabe said, "I exercise three times a week and usually eat very little red meat ... I don't see what else I can do."

Yvonne thought to herself, "Arguing already!" Giving him an exasperated look, she said, "Well, you had normal levels of cholesterol last year, so it *must* be lifestyle. Unless you can think of anything else that's causing it?"

"I know I'm eating better now than I was a year ago," explained Gabe.

"You may think you're eating better, but these tests don't lie. I suggest you begin taking a cholesterol-reducing medication—that way you can still eat whatever you believe is healthy and we'll get that level down below 200."

By now Gabe felt irritated and pressured by the conversation—Yvonne seemed completely unwilling to explore other options. He said, "I don't like the idea of taking drugs. I've been reading about possible side effects."

"And where did you find this information?" asked Yvonne.

"On the Web," said Gabe.

Yvonne shook her head in disbelief. "You should know better than to believe what you read on the Web. I haven't seen anyone develop any ill effects from any of these drugs."

By now Gabe felt very defensive; he said, "But you wouldn't necessarily know what happens to people a few years later. I just want to look at some alternatives."

Yvonne was also becoming increasingly exasperated. "Well, what exactly do you want to do then? You *do* need to reduce your cholesterol level and I've told you what I think."

"I read that the 200 cutoff figure is somewhat arbitrary—and doesn't correlate with people who actually have heart disease," said Gabe defiantly.

"Oh, did you read that on the Web, too?" snapped Yvonne.

The appointment ended with Gabe reluctantly agreeing to reexamine his diet. Gabe left feeling unheard and discounted; Yvonne, on the other hand, now had an even more entrenched negative point of view about Gabe.

Switch Filters

I do not like this person. I must get to know him better. —Abraham Lincoln

The alternative to listening through a negative filter is listening through a filter of collaboration. This means choosing to switch the focus of your attention to both what the other person needs and what qualities you can bring that will help improve the situation. This switching of filters is like shining a flashlight in a dark room—you will illuminate wherever you choose to focus the light. (If you absolutely can't live without your negative filter, you can always switch back to it when the need for collaboration has passed.)

Negative filters are persistent and usually don't disappear overnight; you may find it necessary to refocus your attention several times during a conversation. There are three key steps to switching from a negative filter to a filter of collaboration:

Step 1: Notice When You Are Listening Through a Negative Filter

Most people have red flags that accompany a negative filter. These may include: a tightness in the shoulders or stomach, a clenching of the jaw, and, of course, gossiping.

Ask yourself: What symptoms commonly warn you that you have a negative filter about someone?

Step 2: Switch Your Attention

Slide the negative filter into the background and bring the alternative filter of collaboration into the foreground. You can do this by switching where you focus your attention. For example, if you're listening to a coworker through a negative "lazy" filter, you'll inevitably interpret everything he or she says or does as evidence of laziness. For example, if your coworker takes a break, it's because he or she "doesn't like working." If your coworker's desk is a mess, it's because he or she is "too lazy to clean it up," and so on.

A better—and less stressful—approach is to become aware that you have a negative filter (step 1) and then refocus (switch) your energy and attention to a filter of collaboration by asking yourself, "What does this person or situation need in order to move forward—and how can I provide it?" Asking yourself this question will immediately shift your attention from the negative to the positive. And then—at least for the duration of the interaction—you'll be able to listen more openly and remain resourceful.

In the case study above, Yvonne never switched from her negative "argumentative" filter about Gabe to a filter of collaboration. If she had silently asked herself the question, "What does Gabe need in order to move forward and how can I provide it?" she might have noticed that Gabe was actually very committed to his own health. He had taken the initiative to research health issues and had made some wise lifestyle changes. Instead, by persistently focusing on Gabe's resistance to her advice, Yvonne prevented herself from identifying other avenues that might have made the conversation more useful and satisfying for them both. Unfortunately, by the end of the appointment Gabe had now developed his own negative "inflexible" filter about Yvonne. The next time they meet (if Gabe doesn't just change medical practitioners), each will come armed with a negative filter and the conversation will be even less productive.

If Yvonne had switched her negative filter to a filter of collaboration, the conversation could have gone quite differently. For example, when Gabe said, "I exercise three times a week and usually eat very little red meat.... I don't see what else I can do," Yvonne could have asked herself, "What do I need to say to Gabe to move this conversation forward in the right direction?" She might then have chosen to praise Gabe's diet and exercise. She could have responded, "That's excellent! Good work! I know it often isn't easy to make these changes. It's obvious that you have a real commitment to your health." Chances are Gabe would then have felt appreciated, not dismissed, and the conversation would have continued in a more positive direction.

Step 3: Focus on Addressing Behaviors

As a rule, negative filters don't just pop up out of thin air. Negative filters tend to be the result of us observing another person doing or saying something repeatedly and then forming a judgment about it. For example, think of a negative "stupid" filter that you've had about someone. What did they say and do that led you to the conclusion that they were stupid? A few of the "stupid" behaviors we often hear described in our workshops are:

- The customer never knows proper procedure and never has the paperwork filled out correctly.

- My coworker gets a blank look when I am explaining something.

- My boss can't remember anything, and asks me the same question over and over.

If you analyze the attributes that make up "stupid"—or any other negative filter—you'll find it's always a set of specific, observable behaviors, not inherent physiological properties. Negative filters are opinions we form about others' behaviors. It's important to learn to distinguish between the behavior and your negative opinion about it. You don't have to give up your negative opinion, just don't focus on it. Instead, pay attention to the specific behaviors you observe and keep asking yourself what you can do to address, resolve, and deal with them.

While you may not always have much control over what goes on in your workplace, you do have control over how you choose to respond (see Choose Choice in chapter 4). By learning and practicing these three key steps, you'll both avoid creating antagonistic relationships and foster more collaboration with those you work with.

STRESS AND NEGATIVE FILTERS

As was obvious in our case study, listening through a negative filter can significantly raise your stress level. Here's why:

At the base of your skull is the hypothalamus gland. Its job is to transform messages sent by the brain into chemical responses for the body. For example, when you're watching a really scary movie, your heart beats faster, your breathing becomes shallow, and you start to perspire. Your mind knows it's just a movie but you respond physically as if you're actually in a real, live, threatening situation. That's the hypothalamus gland in action.

The hypothalamus doesn't distinguish between what's real and what's imagined. Moreover, it makes no distinction between our opinions about people (he's a jerk) and what is really true (I *think* he's a jerk). For example, think of a time when you lay in bed almost asleep, and then began worrying about something that might possibly happen in the future. Before you knew it, you were probably wide-awake—heart pounding, adrenaline rushing—and all just the result of your thoughts! Because the hypothalamus reacts as if your thoughts, opinions, and negative filters are reality, it sets about preparing your body for conflict by producing cortisol, a chemical that increases blood sugar and speeds up the body's metabolism.

Summary

➤ Work requires us to collaborate with different types of people, which leads to the benefit of greater diversity.

➤ Initial negative reactions can turn into negative filters; a negative filter is a persistent negative point of view about another person.

➤ Negative filters are contagious; we pass them on to other people, often without even realizing it.

➤ The more we focus on our negative filter of another person, the harder it is for us to create collaboration with him or her.

➤ Switching to a filter of collaboration means changing the focus of your attention from your opinion of the other person to what they need and what positive qualities you can bring to the situation.

➤ The three key steps to switching from a negative filter to a filter of collaboration are:

  › **Step 1:** Notice when you are listening through a negative filter.

  › **Step 2:** Switch your attention to a filter of collaboration.

  › **Step 3:** Focus on addressing behaviors.

CHAPTER 12

THE INS AND OUTS OF ANGER

Regina, a project manager with a financial firm, was doing everything she knew to effectively deal with her anger over a work situation—but it wasn't getting any better. As the weeks went by, she became increasingly angry, frustrated, and depressed.

One day, while talking to a close friend about the situation, a light bulb went off in Regina's head: she realized that she needed to handle her anger more from the inside-out and less from the outside-in.

Many people are skilled at controlling the outward expressions of anger: they may have learned to modulate the tone of their voice to sound more calm and neutral, or they may understand how to choose words and phrases that are less threatening to the listener (e.g., "I messages" versus "you messages"; see chapter 10, Facing Tense Times)—or they may simply use good judgment in determining when is or isn't a good time to express their feelings.

Smart people excel at managing their anger both externally and internally. They have learned how to deal with the anger they feel by going beyond it to the emotions that lay beneath (sadness, loss of control, etc.). Smart people are able to calm themselves down and let go of their anger more quickly.

ANGER HURTS

Ticked off, angry, upset, hostile, irritated, annoyed, resentful, frustrated, bitter, and bitchy—these are just a few of the descriptions we have for our manifestations of anger. Ranging from a slight irritation to a burning rage, anger, even in its mildest forms, can have a powerful impact on our physical health, mental state, emotional well-being, and relationships with others.

Anger stimulates the fight-or-flight response, which causes the release of the hormones adrenaline, noradrenaline, epinephrine, and norepinephrine into the blood stream. In turn, these hormones increase blood pressure and heart rate while simultaneously contracting blood vessels.

The long-term—and very serious—effects of chronic intense anger (as opposed to infrequent mild anger) are well researched and documented. Studies going back as far as 1942 have linked chronic suppressed anger with hypertension and chronic expressed anger with heart disease. One long-term study by the Johns Hopkins University School of Medicine (2002) reported that young men with high levels of anger in response to stressful situations were six times more likely than their less angry colleagues to have a heart attack by age 55, regardless of family history. Other effects of anger include lost sleep, depression, lashing out, overeating, overdrinking, and overworking.

Desk Rage on the Rise

Slamming down the phone, yelling at coworkers, giving the computer (or copier) a good whack, shouting profanities, and throwing papers in frustration—psychologists may call this *counterproductive workplace behavior*, but in more down-home terms it's known as *desk rage*.

Regardless of what name it is called, one thing seems clear: worldwide, workplace outbursts of anger are on the rise. In a national survey of American workers done by Integra Realty Resources in 2000, 42 percent surveyed reported that yelling and verbal abuse were common occurrences in their workplace, 29 percent acknowledged having yelled at coworkers, and 14 percent said that equipment or machinery had been damaged as a result of an angry employee.

A survey of 1,500 workers by the University of North Carolina Kenan-Flagler Business School in 1999 found that 12 percent of those surveyed had quit a job at some point to avoid nasty people at work and 45 percent were thinking about doing so. Moreover, more than half of those interviewed reported losing time at work worrying about others' rude behavior toward them.

The Anatomy of Anger

Imagine that it's Wednesday morning and your coworker Jennifer still hasn't given you the research she promised you for your report that's due Friday. You may take this to mean that Jennifer is being disrespectful to you and doesn't care about the report. "She's always doing this!" you say to yourself. "How can she be so inconsiderate of my time?" When you see her next you'll probably give her the cold shoulder.

But what if there was another possibility? Maybe Jennifer emailed the research to you but it didn't get through; maybe someone in her family is ill and she hasn't been able to get to it; maybe she's putting the finishing touches on the research today, even as you gnash your teeth in frustration. At this point in the situation you really don't have enough information to know if your anger is warranted.

"We very rapidly make sense of a situation, like pushing a button on a camera," says social psychologist Kenneth Sole. "And once we do, if we interpret what happened in a negative way, things can very quickly move in an angry direction."

Trigger Thoughts

In the example above, Jennifer's not getting the research to you is what psychologists call a *trigger situation*, which leads to *trigger thoughts*, which leads to angry feelings—which can lead to angry behavior. We all have hot buttons that when pushed can make us feel and act in an angry way. Learning to identify and unhook yourself from trigger situations and thoughts is the first step to breaking the cycle of anger.

According to Peaco Todd, coauthor of *The Ultimate Guide to Transforming Anger* (2004), "Workplace anger most often arises from feelings of powerlessness: over uncooperative or incompetent coworkers, over feelings of injustice or inequity, and over unfair expectations on the part of those in authority."

We have interviewed and talked with thousands of people about what makes them angry at work. Here is a sample of some common trigger situations and thoughts (can you relate to any of these?):

Frances, a dermatologist: *People have always told me—and I've always known it about myself—that I don't suffer fools gladly. My perception of other people's incompetence is a definite hot button when it comes to getting angry.*

Kevin, an accountant: *I often see myself as working harder and caring more about getting the job done well than many of my coworkers. This is often a cause of my anger at work.*

Rob, an art director: *People who aren't organized and efficient end up taking up my valuable time. This makes me angry.*

Gina, a project manager: *Sometimes my boss asks me to do something in a very specific way, but then when it's done he says it's not what he expected or wanted. I get angry because although I'm the one who ends up blamed, the real problem is he didn't communicate clearly.*

Regardless of the forms they may take, trigger situations—and the corresponding thinking patterns underneath—are much of what causes us to get angry. This doesn't mean that our anger is never justified. In the real world at work, we *are* sometimes treated unfairly, we *are* occasionally disrespected by coworkers, bosses, and customers, and we *are* from time to time wronged. Feelings of anger in these situations are understandable, particularly when they mobilize us to protect ourselves in healthy and effective ways by doing something about the situation. However, focusing on trigger thoughts can lead to an unhealthy anger, in which we tell ourselves we are helpless, the other person is causing us to suffer, and we won't be out of pain until they change.

According to psychologist Matthew McKay, "You can always tell unhealthy anger because it involves a lot of complaining, passive-aggressive behaviors, and a 'victim' mentality. With healthy anger the person takes responsibility for doing something about the situation and chooses effective strategies to get out of the pain they are feeling."

FROM HOT TO COLD: STRATEGIES FOR LETTING GO

While we may have a legitimate reason to get angry in the first place, staying angry past the point of effective expression or action is harmful. However, many of us perpetuate our anger: we get mad and then stay mad. In particular, the stories we tell ourselves often actually increase our anger about a given situation. Even if the circumstances are real and valid, all that may stand in the way of moving past the anger may be what we ourselves are doing to keep it going.

There's an important difference between condoning another's behavior and letting go of our anger. Managing our own anger does not eliminate the need to deal with the effects of the other person's actions. Managing our anger means recognizing that the energy being spent in remaining angry will not fix the situation—and is hurting us (usually far more than it's hurting them).

YOUR HOT BUTTONS

Knowing what your trigger thoughts are is essential for preventing unhealthy anger and reducing the reasonable anger you may experience. Think about a situation in the recent past that made you angry. What thoughts or themes of thought triggered your anger? What did you tell yourself about the other person or situation? What did you say about yourself? For example:

"This isn't fair."

"This shouldn't be taking so long."

"She should know better than to act like this."

"I really screwed up."

How often do you find that these types of thoughts are the precursors to your anger? Once you know what your hot buttons are, you can create coping actions and thoughts that will help reduce or eliminate the hold these trigger thoughts have on you.

CASE STUDY: Trina and the Inconsiderate Actor

Trina, a professional actress, was cast in a play she had always wanted to perform. She loved her role and was really looking forward to the experience. However, a few weeks into rehearsals she began having problems with a fellow actor. She found his behavior unprofessional and inconsiderate. She felt like she was always having to work around his rudeness, mistakes, and ego.

"I had so much anger and frustration towards this person that it was affecting my health," says Trina. "I was having trouble sleeping and I was becoming distracted and depressed. I just could not seem to let go of the anger I felt. I went to see a therapist who pointed out that the anger was hurting me and suggested I find a way to let go of it. Intellectually I understood what the therapist was saying, but my question was *how* do you do that?"

Core Thinking Patterns

Smart people know the kinds of thoughts to stay away from—smart people are aware of the core thinking patterns that can keep them stuck feeling angry. By understanding these patterns of anger you, too, can learn to let go of your anger and put your energy into more constructive places.

Falling into Always/Never

One problematic thinking pattern is to overly generalize what has happened, magnifying or minimizing to an extreme. For example, thinking, "He is *always* interrupting me!" Or, "He *never* says thank you!" Or, "I am *always* having to work around his mistakes!" Or, "*Nothing* is ever good enough for him!" These types of all-or-nothing statements are so general they blind us from the more accurate description of what is actually going on.

Minimize this behavior by speaking and thinking as accurately and factually as possible about the situation. For example, "At Friday's rehearsal, he complained about how late we seemed to be going." Specifics and actualities more accurately pinpoint the source of anger and make it easier to deal with.

Accentuating the Negative

A second problematic thinking pattern is to discount anything positive about the person or situation and focus only on the negative. A myopic focus on things that are wrong or not working —without any acknowledgement of what is right and working— can cement angry feelings in place.

Break free from this negative cycle by being willing to acknowledge something positive about the person or situation. Of course, when you're ready to tear your hair out, this can be challenging! Start with something small that you can easily see. For example, "At Friday's rehearsal, he was getting a cup of tea and asked me if I would like one, too." Just by acknowledging small, positive aspects, you can help yourself broaden your perspective.

Assigning Labels

A third problematic thinking pattern is to make sweeping, big picture assertions about the other person's character based on their behavior. For example, thinking, "He is so selfish!" Or, "She's a control freak!" Or, "My boss is a jerk." (For a more detailed account of how negative filters work, see chapter 11.) While we may feel strongly that the label we have attached to the person is accurate, it nonetheless encourages us to focus on our negative opinion of the person—instead of on taking steps to resolve the behavior.

Focusing on specific behaviors can counterbalance assigning labels. Ask yourself, "What happened?" "When and how often does it happen?" And, "How does it affect me?" For example, instead of thinking, "He is so rude," focus on the specific relevant behavior: "He took up the whole left side of the dressing room," and what you can do to resolve and address it.

Dwelling on Blame

A fourth problematic thinking pattern is to allow yourself to feel that the other person is entirely responsible for whatever has happened and you are merely a victim. The real problem here is that blaming takes all the power out of your hands and transfers it to the person or situation making you angry. Of course, there are times when another person *is* responsible for a hurt or injustice we have suffered, and it's important that we acknowledge this; however, continuing to dwell on blame is unhealthy.

The solution is to switch your attention to focusing on fixing the problem, rather than on apportioning the blame. Create a plan to take care of yourself regardless of what else is happening and don't put your hopes into the other person or situation changing or doing something different.

Assigning Motives

A fifth problematic thinking pattern is to jump to conclusions about another person's reasons for doing what they've done. More often than not, we really just don't know. For example, we may tell ourselves another person's dismissive behavior is because he or she doesn't respect us, but it could just as easily be because his or her mother refused to buy the little red wagon they wanted at age five! The key to getting out of assigning motives is to focus on how the other person's behavior affects you and what you can do about it.

Revisiting the Experience

A sixth problematic thinking pattern is to mentally keep the experience—and the anger—alive. For example, you're revisiting the experience too often if you find yourself venting your anger to anyone who will listen, over and over again.

One way professional athletes train is by repeatedly imagining the action they want to perform, e.g., a perfect golf swing. This works because our body doesn't know that we aren't really experiencing the situation—our body reacts as if the situation is real. Similarly—and much less positively!—every time we revisit our anger, we reinforce our negative feelings.

There are times when you will need to vent to a friendly listener as a way to get the frustration you feel out of your system. The difference between complaining and communicating is the intention you have to let it go once you have gotten it out. (For more information on communicating frustration, check out chapter 13: Speak Up and Be Heard.)

The Prevailing Wisdom: Five Practices

We interviewed a variety of experts in the field of anger management and gleaned from them five helpful practices for managing your anger. The practices may seem obvious, but that does not necessarily mean they are easy! However, putting them into practice can make a world of difference in how you experience and manage your anger.

1. Unpack Your Anger

Alyse Danis, a practicing psychotherapist in San Francisco, emphasizes that anger is never just one emotion or one color: if your anger is red, look for the pink. Dr. Danis (personal communication) explains, "You can unpack your anger by looking for the emotional components that lie underneath (sadness, shame, guilt, loss, etc.). Unpacking is a critical step in being able to move to acceptance (i.e., these are the facts) and resolution (i.e., this is life, things happen)."

The next time you are angry, ask yourself: What other emotions are at play here? What are the feelings underneath the anger that I need to acknowledge?

2. Use Relaxation Techniques

Meditation, deep breathing, exercise, visualization, self-hypnosis, biofeedback—the list goes on. Simple relaxation tools that can help reduce angry feelings are in abundant supply: If you do a Google search for "relaxation techniques" over 5 million search results are listed. Similarly, if you look up the word "stress" on Amazon.com, close to 15,000 books come up, all containing information on relaxation techniques. The key is learning to integrate these techniques into your daily life, so that when faced with a stressful situation they are readily available.

3. Delay Responding

How many times have you said something in the heat of the moment that you later regretted? Reacting on the spot when you're angry denies you the chance to think through what you are feeling, what you need, what you want to say, and how you want to say it. Learn to buy yourself some time to reflect and then respond by using phrases like, "That is something I will have to think about," and, "I'm not sure how to respond to what you just said."

4. Prepare in Advance

In *The Anger Control Workbook* (2000), psychologists Matthew McKay and Peter Rogers discuss a powerful anger management technique they call *anger inoculation*. The technique focuses on a structured mental rehearsal of those coping thoughts and relaxation techniques you want to use in response to imagined anger scenes. By envisioning yourself in the situation and using various coping skills to remain calm, you rehearse *not* getting angry when you are in the actual situation.

For example, let's say you have a client presentation scheduled that you're dreading. In the past, no matter how hard you have worked, the client has always seemed to focus on some small detail he or she dislikes rather than praise you for the overall excellence of your work—just thinking about being in this situation again makes your blood boil!

Using the anger inoculation technique described by McKay and Rogers, you would imagine the upcoming meeting in your mind. What can you see, hear, and touch? What feelings, reactions, and thoughts do you have about this? As you envision it, on a scale of 0-100, how angry is this situation making you? Now, imagine using your coping strategies to diffuse the intensity and amount of anger you feel. Is the anger you feel diminishing? Has it increased? Keep trying out various coping strategies in your mind, until your anger has lessened. By running the scenario and your responses in your head in advance, you can thus remove the sting of surprise and practice keeping a cool head in a hot situation.

5. Revise Your Expectations

One of the biggest sources of anger is unmet expectations. We get angry with ourselves when we don't live up to our own expectations; we get angry at others when they don't believe, act, or behave as we think they should; and we get angry when circumstances don't turn out the way we planned. For example, if you have an expectation that you should be able to get through the airline ticket counter line in ten minutes and it takes thirty, you may get upset.

While many of our expectations may be reasonable, we often continue to hold onto them in situations where past experience has taught us that—though undeniably reasonable—they probably won't be met.

> **Robert, a software engineer:** *I was in a meeting the other day with a coworker I find particularly difficult to work with. In the middle of the meeting, she brought up an item that was on her personal agenda, but not slated to be discussed that day. This is not unusual—she frequently does this. Of course it took up time, irritated the group, etc. After the meeting, I was surprised and angry that she did this, even though she has been asked not to. My expectation was that she would get the message and stop. Finally I have realized that this is just what she does—and it may never stop. I still don't like it, but since I have no power in this situation to stop it, I now expect it and if she does interrupt with her agenda item, I am less upset by it and just deal with it.*

By being aware of our expectations and revising them when appropriate, we are better able to manage our reactions. This doesn't mean condoning behaviors, conditions, or situations that frustrate us; it means telling the truth to ourselves about the nature of what we are dealing with.

FIVE MINUTES TO A CALMER YOU

Even when your anger is justified, suppressing it or expressing it in a destructive way is harmful. The eight steps outlined below are a great practice for calming yourself down.

Step 1: Take a few deep breaths and count to ten.

Step 2: Ask yourself: What are you feeling? What emotions are you are experiencing? Explore beyond the tip of the emotional iceberg—what are you feeling underneath?

Step 3: Ask yourself: What is it about this situation—specifically—that is making you feel angry? What are the circumstances?

Step 4: Ask yourself: What are you telling yourself about this person or situation? What trigger thoughts are you having?

Step 5: Spend thirty seconds thinking of a less personal/more positive reason why the person may be acting this way (or why this situation is the way it is).

Step 6: Substitute your crazy-making thoughts for calming ones. We asked our clients to tell us what calming thoughts they have found particularly useful in dealing with anger on the job. The answers we heard the most often included:

"This will pass."

"Take this one step at a time."

"I am not going to be the victim of these circumstances."

"I am angry and I can take care of this."

"Focus on what I have to get done and do it."

"Where is the humor in this situation?"

Step 7: Ask yourself: What outcome are you looking for? What do you want to have happen (or have stop happening) in the situation?

Step 8: Ask yourself: What actions can you take to achieve your objective?

Use problem-solving methods such as communication, negotiation, leverage, etc. (For more detailed information on how to communicate while angry, check out chapter 13: Speak Up and Be Heard.)

Summary

► Smart people are good at managing their anger both externally and internally; smart people understand both how to control the outward expressions of their anger and how to calm themselves down and cope with the internal aspects of their anger.

► Long-term anger has a serious impact on our physical and mental health; effects include: lost sleep, depression, lashing out, overeating, overdrinking, and overworking.

► The cycle of anger starts with a trigger situation, which leads to trigger thoughts, which lead to angry feelings —which can lead to angry behavior; smart people know how to unhook themselves from trigger thoughts to break the cycle.

► Core thinking patterns are what keep us stuck in anger; these patterns include:

  › Falling into always/never

  › Accentuating the negative

> › Assigning labels

> › Dwelling on blame

> › Assigning motives

> › Revisiting the experience

► The five practices for managing anger are:

1. Unpack your anger

2. Use relaxation techniques

3. Delay responding

4. Prepare in advance

5. Revise your expectations

► All it takes is a focused five minutes to make a difference in calming down.

CHAPTER 13

SPEAK UP AND BE HEARD

In the previous chapters we've largely focused on savvy skills that smart people employ when communicating with someone who is upset or angry. In this chapter we reverse the situation and look at what it takes to successfully have a difficult conversation with a coworker, customer, or boss.

On the surface, this type of communication seems like it should be easier: because you are the one with something to say, you can be proactive rather than reactive, you can prepare what you want to say and how you want to say it, and you can choose the best time to communicate. However, for many people, just the prospect of initiating a difficult conversation is so scary that staying silent is the preferred alternative.

Not expressing our feelings and thoughts protects us from the fear and discomfort of an unfavorable reaction. For example, your coworker may get bent out of shape if you offer some constructive criticism, or your boss may get defensive if you make a small suggestion at the big meeting. Most people shy away from confrontation. However, as uncomfortable as these situations may seem, smart people know that the cost of not speaking up comes with a much higher price tag.

THE COST OF REMAINING SILENT

Everyone has a unique contribution to make in the workplace. In spite of task-filled days, endless meetings, and the too-much-to-do-in-too-little-time syndrome, most of us want to feel like we make a difference at work. Speaking up makes us feel a little more significant, a little more visible in the grinding blur of business life. *Not* speaking up and being heard is equivalent to saying that our opinion doesn't matter, that what we have to contribute is of no consequence—that, essentially, our feelings and thoughts don't count.

According to James Pennebaker, author of *Opening Up: The Healing Power of Expressing Emotions* (1997), there are health costs associated with not speaking up. Dr. Pennebaker and two of his colleagues conducted a study to find out what—if anything—occurs physically when humans suppress emotional issues. The study revealed that the immune system's soldier count (number of lymphocytes and T-helper cells) went down dramatically when emotions were suppressed. By contrast, people taught various techniques designed to resolve emotional issues experienced a boost to their immune system's efficiency.

In addition, not saying what is on our mind can breed resentment—a relationship killer in both

---

THE SOUND OF SILENCE

Take a moment and think of a time when you didn't speak up about a situation that was bothering you—maybe the actions of a coworker, something your boss said, etc. How did it feel to suppress your feelings and communication? How did you eventually resolve the situation?

Next, take a moment and think of a time when you *did* speak up about a situation that was bothering you. How did that feel?

What we communicate is rarely the problem; it's how we communicate it—silently or directly—that's significant.

the workplace and at home. If you're angry but don't speak up, the chances are your anger will leak out as resentment. Basil Fawlty, the John Cleese character in the British TV comedy "Fawlty Towers," was the quintessence of resentment—always making faces at his wife behind her back, using a derisive tone with customers, and being bitingly sarcastic with his staff. Due to its covert nature, resentment never opens itself to discussion or dialogue. Anger, responsibly communicated, can lead to resolution. Resentment, endless and internalized, merely creates a vicious cycle—more and more resentment.

CASE STUDY: Gail and Her Supervisor

Gail is a mechanic at a large truck repair center. Three weeks ago she took a few days of vacation time. But when she returned to work, things weren't quite the same. Here is Gail's version of what happened.

"I am so frustrated. A couple of weeks ago I took a few days off. I hadn't taken a vacation in what seems like forever and I needed some time to relax and enjoy myself. The day I came back to work I was actually a bit excited about seeing everyone and jumping back into things. After I clocked in I went to find my supervisor and say hello. He barely even looked at me—he just said, "I hope you're well rested because your next job is a big one." Sure enough, my whole shift was spent working on a truck that had lots of problems. I managed to muscle my way through it but ever since then I've been getting the worst jobs. I am not exaggerating! Every bad job ends up being mine. The problem is my supervisor. I thought we got along fine, but he's hardly said a word to me in two weeks. This is what I get for taking time off. It would be better if they just told us the truth about vacation time: that we can't really take it without being punished and made to pay for it later!"

At this point Gail wondered how she could possibly speak up and talk to her supervisor about the situation without causing an even worse mess. Smart people know that there are certain steps you can take to help ensure that you speak up and are heard in a way that brings resolution to the situation and minimizes conflict, argument, and bad feelings. Let's explore these steps, using Gail's situation as an example.

Step 1: Separate Fact from Fiction

In the case study above, the story that Gail is telling herself is riddled with fictional elements. Most of us have a blind spot when it comes to separating the actual facts from our opinions, assumptions, and judgments. However, it's important to distinguish between the actual facts and our interpretations so that we are able to deal with what is really going on—not what we think is going on. If we take what Gail says to herself and rigorously separate facts from fiction, we are left with:

Fact: Gail is frustrated.

Fiction: Gail is being punished because she took some time off.

Fact: Gail has been doing some difficult jobs lately.

Fiction: Gail's supervisor has been deliberately giving her bad jobs.

Fact: Gail hasn't had much conversation with her supervisor in two weeks.

Fiction: Gail's supervisor is deliberately not speaking with Gail because he is upset Gail took vacation time.

Step 2: Speak Honestly, Responsibly, and with Good Intent

In chapter 4 we spoke about creating meaningful contexts—a way of viewing circumstances and situations that promotes prospering. In this step, smart people take a similar approach by choosing a positive context or outcome, rather than a negative one, to help guide their difficult conversations. For example, a negative context Gail might have for the conversation she wants to initiate with her supervisor could be, "I am going to make sure my supervisor knows how angry I am that he is punishing me for taking time off." On the other hand, a positive context Gail might have is, "I want to resolve my feelings of frustration so I enjoy my work again."

By separating the facts from the fiction (step 1), and creating a positive context, when Gail speaks to her supervisor she will be more able to honestly say what is true for her—without exaggeration or blame. For example, Gail might say, "I feel really frustrated with the jobs I've been getting lately, they all seem to be hard, and we haven't had much chance to talk over the past few weeks. Can we set up a time to discuss this?" Rather than, "I am really upset. Why have you been giving me all the bad jobs these past few weeks and then ignoring me when I try to talk about it with you? Am I being punished for taking a few days off for vacation or what?"

Clearly, these different approaches will yield different results. Dealing with the issue in a win-lose fashion may at least nominally resolve the situation—but also lead to alienation, conflict, and bad feelings. On the other hand, if Gail speaks responsibly—without blame or negative judgments—her supervisor will be less defensive during the conversation, and the long-term effects more positive. However, for this approach to work, Gail must want to both resolve the problem *and* maintain a good relationship with her supervisor.

Step 3: Plan Your Conversation

Smart people plan their important conversations. Just as you use a recipe to cook a meal or a blueprint to build a house, knowing and planning what you want to say supports a successful outcome to your conversation.

The following checklist is useful as a guide for preparing for a difficult conversation. Take a moment and think of a difficult conversation you need to have with someone and then answer the following questions:

1. What is the core message you want to communicate?

2. What are the relevant and important facts that relate to your core message?

3. What are your strongest emotions/feelings relating to this message?

4. What is the positive context for this conversation?

5. What is the outcome you intend for this conversation?

Reflecting on the above questions, Gail came up with these answers:

1. Core Message: *I think that I'm being penalized for taking vacation time. I want to find out if this is true.*

2. Relevant Facts: *I've been getting really awful jobs to work on ever since I got back and my supervisor hasn't spoken to me much.*

3. Emotions/Feelings: *I feel frustrated and annoyed— and a little bit sad and lonely at being ignored.*

4. Positive Context: *I want to have this conversation so I feel good when I come to work*

5. Intended Outcome: *I want to feel like I belong at work and that I'm on good terms with my supervisor.*

Just the act of answering the questions itself has given Gail a new way of looking at the issues: now Gail feels less antagonistic toward her supervisor and more open to resolving the situation.

Step 4: Use Your Pause and Resume Buttons

Conversations are organic and spontaneous—no matter how much planning you do, the actual conversation will be like a fluid dance in which you listen and respond. Sometimes things can get just plain confusing! The conversation may not follow a straight path and the other person may bring up issues that are important to talk about yet not directly related to the focus of your message. By using your mental pause button, you can briefly talk about an important side issue. Once the side issue has been discussed, use your mental resume button to go back to the main conversation where you left off.

For example, in Gail's situation, the conversation could easily spin off into talking about, say, the vacation policy and how it needs to be changed. While this is certainly an important issue, it's not directly connected to what Gail is speaking up about. However, Gail could momentarily pause the central conversation to talk with her supervisor about changing the vacation policy, and then resume her focus on her own experience once they've finished discussing the side issue.

Step 5: Be Smart About Time and Place

Lastly, give some thought to when and where you want to have the conversation. Busy work areas, corridors, and elevators are *not* recommended. If possible, pick a time when the interruptions will be minimal and choose a location that is both private and quiet.

Also, pay attention to the mood of the other person. If they are in a good mood—happy, relaxed, joking, etc.—seize the opportunity for conversation. We all listen better when we feel good. However, if the other person is in a bad mood—angry, frustrated, pressured, etc.—postpone the conversation until a later time. Negative moods narrow how well we listen to other people.

Putting It All Together

Now let's revisit Gail as she has her conversation with her supervisor. She asked for a meeting a couple of days ago, and suggested an off-peak time. Her supervisor agreed, and suggested they meet in his office. Gail entered the office.

"Is this still an okay time?" asked Gail.

"Sure," said her supervisor. "What's on your mind?"

Gail took a seat and said, "Well, as you know I took a few days off a couple of weeks back and since then I've been concerned."

"What about?" asked her supervisor.

"Well," said Gail, "I've been getting a feeling that I did something wrong."

The supervisor seemed surprised. "What? Why?"

"Ever since I got back it seems like I've landed all the crummy jobs," said Gail. "One after the other. I wanted to have this meeting to find out if something is going on."

"Nothing's going on," said the supervisor. "We've just had a lot of tricky vehicles to service. You should be happy that we're so busy. Our competitor's been laying people off because they're so slow. Did you know that?"

"No," said Gail.

The supervisor said, "Yes, they've laid off about twenty people—mostly service engineers. Our regional office told me that we might be buying them out in the very near future."

At this point, Gail noticed that the conversation had taken a side road. She used her pause button to put her issue on hold for a moment, and asked, "Would that mean we'd move to their location or vice versa?"

"I don't know," said the supervisor, "it's really too early to say. How would you feel about changing locations if we decided to move you over there?"

"I'd have to think about it—but it would probably be okay," said Gail.

Seeing this as an opportunity for advancement, Gail wanted to find out more—however, this wasn't what she came to talk about! She now pressed her mental resume button and refocused on her central concerns: "Don't get me wrong, I'm happy for the work, but it seems to me that I've been doing more of the tough vehicles than anyone else. Plus I feel like you haven't said much to me since I got back."

"Gail," said the supervisor, "I've been really busy trying to get my boss the numbers she needs for regional. Like I said, they are seriously looking at a buyout and I've been tasked with coming up with a headcount plan for operating two service centers. I couldn't say anything until the deal was formalized. And I gave you those tough jobs because I know you will do good work even when the conditions are less than ideal. Does that answer your question?"

"I need to ask one more thing," said Gail.

"Go right ahead."

"Do you or the company have a problem with employees taking vacation time when we're really busy?" asked Gail.

The phone rang. The supervisor said, "I have to take this."

"Okay." Gail used the time to reflect on the conversation. The conversation seemed to be flowing easily and she felt much more at ease than when she began. She saw that much of what she had thought was true was really just a fabrication of her own mind.

The supervisor put down the phone. "Sorry about that. So where were we?"

"I was asking if there's a problem taking time off when we're busy," said Gail.

"Well," said the supervisor, "it's never easy having people out when the bays are at capacity, but that's just the way it is. I've never had a problem with it. Now, I have another meeting to go to. Anything else?"

"No, that was it," said Gail. "Thanks for your time."

Her supervisor smiled. "You're welcome, Gail. I appreciate you coming to talk to me and clearing up the confusion."

Gail walked back to her work area feeling ten tons lighter. She couldn't believe the conversation went so well! She saw that the story she'd been telling herself about being penalized was just that—a story that she'd made up. She also saw how her carefully considered, positive, fact-and-feeling-based approach had worked—and kept her supervisor from taking a defensive stance. She had successfully said exactly what was on her mind without trying to set the blame on anyone. She felt proud of herself for having the courage to speak up and be heard.

STAGES OF CONVERSATION

Smart people know that communication is usually the best tool for solving problems at work. But what about those times when a conversation—even a carefully considered, positive, fact-and-feeling-based conversation—doesn't seem to change the situation or make any noticeable difference? Eventually we usually speak up again—we have another conversation with the person in question and reiterate what we said the first time around, except this time we're more frustrated and upset. Then, if nothing changes as a result of this second conversation, we get even more upset and have yet another, often heated, discussion in which we re-reiterate what we said in the first and second conversations.

To *effectively* speak up about something that has not been resolved in prior conversations you must be aware (and willing) to have three different stages of conversation:

Stage 1 Conversation: What happened?

Stage 2 Conversation: Why does it keep happening?

Stage 3 Conversation: How is it impacting the relationship?

Stage 1 Conversation: What happened?

This is the first conversation you have about the topic you want to discuss. Let's say that you're unhappy with a coworker because he or she has time management issues and often asks you to pick up the slack created by his or her own bad planning, and you're fed up with it. Your first conversation would focus on explaining the overall issue from your point of view, hearing what your coworker has to say about it, and coming to some agreement on how things should be handled in the future. If this conversation does the trick and your colleague gets his or her act together, congratulations! However, let's say the situation continues—then it is time to move on to a stage 2 conversation:

Stage 2 Conversation: Why does it keep happening?

Rather than just rehashing and repeating the points from the first conversation, this conversation requires switching subjects and talking about how the last conversation and subsequent strategy seem to have made no difference. This conversation should focus on why the promises, commitments, and attempts to deal with the problem fell through—and what measures can be taken to remedy the situation. If you and your colleague agree on a strategy and the plan works, congratulations! If not, it's time to move on to stage 3:

Stage 3 Conversation: How is it impacting the relationship?

At this point, the conversation is no longer about the content of the situation, it's about the impact that the continued issue is having on your relationship with the other person. This third conversation is about your values and integrity more than anything else. You might explain how you are finding it difficult to trust what your coworker says, how he or she is not respecting your time, or how tired you are of helping him or her when they do not seem to be helping themselves. It can be challenging, but it is often necessary if you want to resolve the issue long-term. Smart people know when it's time to go beyond the content of the situation to having a conversation about the relationship.

Summary

➤ Speaking up helps us realize the unique contributions we make at work; *not* speaking up implies—to ourselves and others—that our opinions do not matter.

➤ Not speaking up when you are angry leads to resentment, a relationship killer at both work and home.

➤ Speak up by:

› Separating the facts from fiction

› Speaking honestly, responsibly, and with good intent

› Planning your conversation

› Using your pause and resume buttons

› Being smart about time and place

➤ If appropriate, be willing to have three stages of conversation:

› **Stage 1:** What happenend?

› **Stage 2:** Why does it keep happening?

› **Stage 3:** How is it impacting the relationship?

THE MINI-MAKEOVERS

Though no one can go back and make a brand new start, anyone can start from now and make a brand new ending.

—Carl Bard

ENDINGS AND BEGINNINGS

Congratulations! You've finished *Watercooler Wisdom: How Smart People Prosper in the Face of Conflict, Pressure, and Change!* Take a few minutes to stand back, reflect, and pat yourself on the back for any changes you've made, goals you've accomplished, or new skills you've acquired from reading this book. Be sure to consider:

- How have your feelings about work changed?

- How have your relationships with coworkers changed?

- What impact has reading this book had on your goals and achieving them?

- What impact has reading this book had on your productivity?

- Which tools do you find yourself using daily/ weekly?

- How have the principles and practices of this book impacted your personal life?

You can use the space below to write down some of your answers:

_____

_____

_____

_____

_____

_____

_____

How does it feel to have accomplished all this? You may find that although you feel satisfied, your internal commentator is saying, "Yeah, but—"

"—I still have a lot of work to do."

"—I wasn't very good at _____."

"—I need to make more progress on _____."

"—I still don't get along with _____."

Don't undermine all your hard work with these negative thoughts! It's important to remember that the process of prospering in the face of conflict, pressure, and change is ongoing. It's like peeling an onion: one layer at a time. The first time you work through this book you learn how to integrate these principles and practices into your life; the second and third time you work through it you'll find yourself working on new and deeper levels.

This book is designed to help you become familiar with the core principles and practices you need for a lifetime of working with greater satisfaction and effectiveness.

We strongly encourage you to review, revisit, and reacquaint yourself with these principles and practices whenever you feel the urge. The more you incorporate them into your daily work life—the more you transform them into regular habits—the better your results will be.

For times when you want to brush up on a specific area, try one of the five mini-makeovers that follow. Each mini-makeover focuses on a core principle covered in the book and shows you how to apply it in sixty minutes or less.

MINI-MAKEOVER 1:
The Energy Booster

This is a great makeover for when you're feeling bogged down, tired, or sluggish—it's a quick pick-me-upper that will give you a much-needed energy burst.

> **Jane, a personal trainer:** *I was working from my home office on a project and found myself unable to focus. I was distracted and in a funky mood. Then I stopped and reflected on why I was feeling so yucky and noticed I had a few nagging incompletions going on! They were all small things—schedule the handyman, drop some clothes off at Goodwill, reply to an email from a colleague, etc.—but they were taking up room in my brain and making me feel antsy. I needed to do something to create some mental space for myself. I stopped what I was doing and gave myself a one-hour time allowance to get as much closure as I could on these nagging items. Once the hour was up I went back to work, feeling lighter and more energized.*

To practice the Energy Booster, stop and make a short list of a few incomplete items that you could finish or partially finish within the next hour. (If you don't have an hour, set your own time limit.) The items you select can be work-related or personal. For example, a phone call you need to make, an email you've been putting off writing, an errand you've been meaning to run, a light bulb that needs changing, papers that should be filed, etc. One tip: the more an item is bugging you, the greater relief you'll feel by getting it done—regardless of size.

The items I want to work on are:

_____

_____

_____

_____

_____

_____

_____

_____

Once you have written your list, take a look at the clock and note the time. Give yourself one hour (or whatever period of time you've designated) to get as many of these items done as possible. As you complete each item check it off your list—and get that *yee-haw!* feeling that comes from finally getting it done!

Take a few minutes to write down how you feel having gained some closure with these items:

_____

_____

_____

_____

_____

_____

MINI-MAKEOVER 2:
The Propeller

Often, there are so many urgent things to do at work we find ourselves focusing only on what needs our immediate attention, while our other, equally important yet less pressing goals fall by the wayside. As a result, we may find it difficult to consistently work on our goals. In our twenty years of consulting, we have observed that consistently working on goals is the key to accomplishing them. This mini-makeover will propel you toward accomplishing your goals. Here's how the Propeller works.

First, identify one goal you would like to move forward with, but which—for whatever reason—you haven't found the time to work on.

The goal I am going to work on is: _____

Next, open your date book (electronic or paper) and schedule some time—yes, actually block out a one-hour time slot!—either today or in the next few days to work on this goal.

The date and time I am committing to working on this goal is:

_____

Next, write down at least three mini-tasks associated with the goal you've picked. Remember: identifying mini-tasks is a great way to break down a larger goal into more bite-sized, doable pieces.

The three mini-tasks related to this goal are:

1. _____

2. _____

3. _____

Review the three items above. If you feel one or more of these mini-tasks can reasonably be done within the hour, great!—you are ready to move on. If not, reduce the chunk size of these mini-tasks into even smaller tasks that you can confidently complete within an hour.

Three even smaller tasks (from one of the above mini-tasks) are:

1. _____

2. _____

3. _____

A few things to keep in mind when the scheduled time arrives for working on your goal:

- Let other people around you (coworkers, family, etc.) know that you'll be working on an important project during that time; ask them not to disturb you, except in cases of emergency.

- Don't answer your phone or email during the designated time! Protect yourself from interruptions that might prevent you from getting your goals accomplished.

- Stay focused: only work on the goal you've chosen; don't get dragged off track by other related (or non-related!) projects, to-do items, etc.

———

MINI-MAKEOVER 3:
The Eye Opener

One of the ways we grow—both at work and in our personal lives—is by receiving feedback, coaching, and advice from others, especially from those we trust and respect. As we have discussed in this book, knowing both how to give and receive feedback is a critical skill. The Eye Opener is a great makeover to use when there is a problem, issue, or situation for which you feel another person's perspective might help. To use the Eye Opener, follow these five steps:

Step 1: Start by directly asking a friend, peer, or coworker for feedback. Pick someone you trust and who you feel has your best interests at heart. (Don't ask someone who might be put in an awkward or conflicted situation by giving you feedback.) Let the person know the issue at hand and what objectives you are looking to achieve. Ask if he or she would be willing to give you honest feedback and observations. Assuming your invitation is accepted, move on to step 2. If the person says no, don't be upset! Remember: people are busy and may be uncomfortable giving feedback. If this happens, simply find someone else you can ask.

Step 2: Once the person accepts your invitation, set a specific date, time, and place—somewhere private—to meet. (If appropriate, you may want to take your advisor out to lunch or coffee for the conversation.) Make sure the person understands enough about the situation before the meeting to be able to think the situation over carefully before actually offering any advice.

Step 3: Meet and listen. When you do get together, listening is your primary job—and it can be quite difficult! Even though you asked for the feedback, you may find that when you hear it, you don't like it. If this is the case, don't hold it against the person who provided it. (Doing so is the quickest way to deny yourself any future honest input.) You don't have to agree or disagree—just take in what your advisor says, ask questions for clarification and further understanding, and, above all, don't get defensive.

Step 4: Soon after the session, send an email or note thanking the person for his or her time and thoughts. Down the road a bit, contact the person again to explain both how you utilized the feedback you received and how the situation worked out.

Step 5: Be willing to do this for other people! If you are lucky enough to be asked for your feedback by someone you work with, treat it with the honor it deserves, and—keeping that person's best interests firmly in your heart—provide any feedback or advice you can.

———

MINI-MAKEOVER 4:
The Filter Fixer

The hardest part about removing a negative filter can be realizing you have one! Often, a filter feels like plain old annoyance or frustration. This mini-makeover will both help you identify when you're trapped in a negative filter and give you more leverage to shift into a filter of collaboration.

By stepping back and taking a look at the make-up of your negative filters, you can gain enough distance to start formulating a plan of attack for filter fixing. The following are six key questions to reflect on and answer:

1. The symptoms I experience with negative filters are:

   _____

   _____

   _____

We all have patterns of symptoms that occur when we are stuck in a negative filter—i.e., grinding our teeth, muttering under our breath, etc. Since more often than not these same symptoms recur, it's important to learn to identify them. The more familiar you are with your particular brand of negative filter behavior, the quicker and easier it will be for you to take notice and then take action.

2. My negative thoughts about this person or situation are:

   _____

   _____

   _____

Be sure to make a complete list—really drain your brain, no matter how petty, rude, or unkind your thoughts may seem. Remember: they're just *horizontal* thoughts.

3.   My negative filter reacts to the following behaviors:

_____

_____

_____

As we learned in chapter 11, negative filters are the result of your opinion of another person's behavior. It is critical to identify the specific, observable behaviors you're reacting to in order to determine other ways you might deal with them. Be rigorous in separating your opinions (he's a jerk!) from the specific actions that are observable (he interrupts me when I talk.).

4.   Some reasons this person might be behaving this way include:

_____

_____

_____

This is a tough one because it can feel as if you're justifying the person being a jerk! Don't worry, you're not—you're looking for any underlying reasons for the person's behavior so that you can embrace an alternative, less fixed, point of view, and, if appropriate, address him or her directly about his or her behavior. You're also learning to develop more compassion and understanding for the person, something we all need more of in today's world.

5. Is there anyone I could talk to who could help me decide how to address the situation, my filter, and/or this person's behavior?

_____

_____

_____

We *aren't* recommending you go around gossiping about the person and spreading your negative filter to others. We *are* recommending that you use the power of collaboration to help you gain perspective on ways of removing your negative filter and addressing the situation!

6. What does this person or situation need in order to move forward—and how can I provide it?

_____

_____

_____

Now that you have taken some time to reflect on the filter, is there any action that would be appropriate for you to take? What can you do—or stop doing—that could keep you from the negative filter's downward spiral? Depending on the strength of the filter, you may have to review these questions several times, over a period of days or weeks, to crack the filter's hold over you.

MINI-MAKEOVER 5:
The Relationship Builder

We once heard a stand-up comedian talking about his work and saying that one of the reasons why he loved his job so much was because on most days he received applause and a standing ovation. "Every day people clap for me—and often they even stand up!" He continued, "Now, most people, they don't get that—rarely do you walk into the office in the morning and everyone you work with stands up, applauding and yelling, 'Yay Jim! Great job on that phone call yesterday!'" As they say, only the truth is funny.

Contribution helps sustain us at work. Feeling that we're making a difference is crucial to a satisfying work life. This mini-makeover helps you get into the habit of recognizing others for what they contribute—which in turn helps you to build stronger and better relationships with those you work with.

We recommend doing this mini-makeover on a regular basis, once every few weeks or so. This is also a great makeover for reestablishing a better coworker relationship when you're feeling a bit out of sync. Use the format of the following five questions (who, what, how, where, and when) to plan and execute the Relationship Builder:

Who? and What?

First, consider whom you want to acknowledge, and for what? Often someone and/or something will come to mind as soon as you ask yourself the question. If this is the case, go with it. Once you develop the habit of looking for things to appreciate in others you'll see opportunities everywhere. Expressing your gratitude for the difference made by your coworkers might sound Pollyanna-ish—and feel a bit embarrassing—but showing appreciation for others is a very simple act that can forge much stronger relationships. Here are some ideas to get you started:

- Was there someone who said or did something in a recent meeting that helped move the group forward, or got the group to think in a new way? Perhaps someone who came up with a good solution to a persistent problem the group had been wrestling with?

- Is there a specific person who has helped you with something recently? Someone who went out of his or her way? Did someone do you a favor, go the extra mile?

- Did someone make a good business connection for you? Or help you to network in some way?

- Do you admire the way someone handled a situation you were a part of? Did someone show a quality you appreciated?

- Is there a person you work with who was kind to you recently?

How?

Acknowledgment can be simple and quick, or take time, effort, and money. How you acknowledge the person depends on what you feel is appropriate to what you are thanking them for. For example, for a coworker who spends a few minutes giving you his or her feedback, an email or a note of thanks would probably be appropriate. On the other hand, for a coworker who spends several hours helping you with a project as a personal favor, lunch or a small gift might be appropriate. In most cases an email, note, or phone call will do the trick.

When? and Where?

Depending on the how you have chosen, the where and when should follow naturally. The closer your thanks come to the actual event, the more impact it will have. Similarly, if you're going to say thank you in person, ensure you have the person's full attention first, so you can be certain he or she is present in spirit as well as body.

REFERENCES

Accountemps. 2003. Study. Menlo Park, Calif.

Bureau of Labor Statistics. http://www.dol.gov/dol/topic/work hours/index.htm (accessed May 17, 2005).

Center for a New American Dream. 2004. Survey. http://www. newdream.org (accessed DATE).

Covey, Stephen R. 1989. *The Seven Habits of Highly Effective People.* New York: Free Press.

Danis. Alyse. April 28, 2005. Personal communication.

Dewey, John. 1997. *How We Think.* Mineola, NY: Dover Publications.

Drucker, Peter F. 1996. *The Effective Executive.* New York: HarperCollins.

ehappylife.com. 2003. Survey: Goal Systems. www.ehappylife. com/custom/pollresult30.html (accessed on May 24, 2005).

Fischer, Norman. 2004. *Taking Our Places.* New York: HarperCollins.

Frost, Robert. 1969. *The Poetry of Robert Frost.* New York: Henry Holt.

Galinsky, Ellen. 2005. Families and Work Institute. New York.

Gallagher, Olive. 2004. *The Nude Ethicist: A Simple Path to the Good Life*. Santa Fe, NM: Rising Moon Press.

The Gallup Organization. 2004. Survey: Are Americans Really Abject Wokaholics?

Geller, Adam. 2005. Survey: Third of Americans are overworked. *USA Today*, March 16.

Hoffman Institute. The Feelings List. San Anselmo, Calif.

Iacocca, Lee. http://www.brainyquote.com/quotes/authors/l/lee_iacocca.html (accessed on July 22, 2005).

Integra Realty Resources. 2001. Study: Stress.

Johns Hopkins University School of Medicine. http://www.sitesupport.org/module1/teacherreflection.htm (accessed April 22, 2005).

Johns Hopkins University School of Medicine. 2002. Study: Anger in young men and subsequent premature cardiovascular disease. *Archives of Internal Medicine*. 162: 901–906.

Johnson, C. Ray. 1998. *CEO Logic: How to Think and Act Like a Chief Executive*. Franklin Lakes, NJ: Career Press.

Juran, Joseph M. 1937. Pareto principle. The Juran Institute. Southbury, Conn.

Kronos Incorporated. 2004. Survey: Working in America: The disgruntled workforce. Chelmsford, Mass.

McKay, Matthew, and Peter D. Rogers. 2000. *The Anger Control Workbook*. Oakland, CA: New Harbinger Publications.

McKay, Matthew, Peter D. Rogers, and Judith McKay. 2003. *When Anger Hurts*. Oakland, CA: New Harbinger Publications.

McKay, Matthew. April 29, 2005. Personal communication.

Middelton-Moz, Jane, Lisa Tener, and Peaco Todd. 2004. *The Ultimate Guide to Transforming Anger*. Deerfield Beach, FL: Health Communications Inc.

Miller, George. 1956. The magical number seven, plus or minus two: Some limits on our capacity for processing information. *The Psychological Review* 63:81–97.

National Mental Health Association. Stress: Coping with everyday problems. http://www.nmha.org/infoctr/factsheets/41.cfm (accessed June 13, 2005).

New American Dream. 2004. Survey: Rethinking the american dream. http://www.newdream.org/newsletter/survey.php (accessed March 6, 2005).

Nightingale, Earl. Nightingale Conant Corporation. Niles, IL.

Pareto, Vilfredo. 1897. Cours d'économie politique.

Pennebaker, James W. 1997. *Opening Up: The Healing Power of Expressing Emotions*. New York: Guilford Press.

Pychyl, Timothy. 2001. Study: Five days of emotion. Ottawa, Canada: Carleton University.

Senge, Peter M. 1994. *The Fifth Discipline*. New York: Currency.

Schwartz, Evan I. 2004. *Juice: The Creative Fuel That Drives World-Class Inventors*. Boston: Harvard Business School Press.

Schwartz, Tony, and Jim Loehr. 2003. *The Power of Full Engagement*. New York: Free Press.

Sole, Kenneth. March 15, 2005. Personal communication.

Szalavitz, Maia. 2003. Stand and deliver. *Psychology Today*, August 26.

Tabakin, Beth. June 10, 2005. Personal communication.

Todd, Peaco. April 28, 2005. Personal communication.

United Nations. 1992. National Report. 20th Century Epidemic.

Wheatley, Margaret. 1994. *Leadership and the New Science*. San Francisco: Berrett-Koehler.

World Heath Organization. 1998. Study: World Wide Epidemic.

ABOUT STERLING CONSULTING GROUP

Sterling Consulting Group is an international management consulting company specializing in the people side of business. Over the past twenty years we have worked throughout the world with such companies as American Express, Apple Computer, Carl Zeiss, Chevron, IBM, Microsoft, Oracle, Roche and Warner Brothers. We offer a variety of programs including:

Keynote Speeches: Karen Leland and Keith Bailey are among the highest-rated presenters on the training/speaking circuit and offer programs that are educational, entertaining, motivational and practical. Suitable for all audiences from Ceo's to sales teams, our presentations are tailored to your group and based on the principles and practices in Watercooler Wisdom.

Training Programs: SCG has trained hundreds of thousands of executives, managers and staff in the people side of business. All of our training programs are customized to reflect your specific needs, concerns and industry. Our programs are highly interactive, creating trainings that are fun, lively, and based on practical real world information that attendees can use immediately. We currently offer a variety of training programs based on the Watercooler Wisdom model.

Watercooler Wisdom Coach Certification: For those interested in coaching others in the principles and practices highlighted in Watercooler Wisdom we offer a certification process. Our program provides both content and structure for a complete coaching process that existing coaches can use with their current clients and new coaches can use to build a practice.

Customized online programs: Utilizing our expertise in the area of course development, we offer web-based training programs that are interactive and engaging. Drawing from the content of Watercool Widsom, as well as our other training programs, we can write, produce and host a customized online training for your organization.

If you are interested in speaking to us about any of the above please contact Karen Leland/ Keith Bailey at:

Sterling Consulting Group, Inc.
180 Harbor Drive #208
Sausalito, CA 94965
Phone: (415) 331-5200
Fax: (415) 331-5272
E-mail: info@scgtraining.com
www.scgtraining.com

In 1986, **Karen Leland** and **Keith Bailey** founded Sterling Consulting Group, Inc. and shortly thereafter made history by being chosen over more than a dozen European competitors to become the first American consulting company to win a major contract for business communication training within the British government.

Over the past twenty years they have worked throughout the United States, Europe, Asia and South America with a diverse list of Fortune 500 companies in such industries as Banking, Transportation, Retail and Telecommunications. Among others their clients include: Arco, Bank of America, Avis Rental Car, Johnson & Johnson, Sprint and Xerox.

They are sought after speakers who provide both motivation and practical hands on information in their presentations. They have spoken for such groups as Young Presidents Organization, The Society of Association Executives, The Society of Consumer Affairs and the Direct Marketing Association among others.

Because of their extensive experience and expertise they have been featured in dozens of magazines and newspapers including: The New York Times, Newsweek and Time. They also have extensive on-air experience and have been interviewed on ABC, CNN, NBC, Fox, The Oprah Winfrey Show and over twenty other affiliates.

In addition to Watercooler Wisdom, They have written several other books including Online Customer Service For Dummies and Customer Service For Dummies, first, second and third editions, which have over 200,000 copies. Their books have been translated into ten other languages including Russian, Korean, Arabic, Spanish and German.

Some Other
New Harbinger Titles

Talk to Me, Item 3317 $12.95

Romantic Intelligence, Item 3309 $15.95

Eating Mindfully, Item 3503 $13.95

Sex Talk, Item 2868 $12.95

Everyday Adventures for the Soul, Item 2981 $11.95

The Daughter-In-Law's Survival Guide, Item 2817 $12.95

Love Tune-Ups, Item 2744 $10.95

Spiritual Housecleaning, Item 2396 $12.95

The 50 Best Ways to Simplify Your Life, Item 2558 $11.95

Brave New You, Item 2590 $13.95

Loving Your Teenage Daughter, Item 2620 $14.95

The Conscious Bride, Item 2132 $12.95

Juicy Tomatoes, Item 2175 $13.95

Facing 30, Item 1500 $12.95

Fifty Great Tips, Tricks, and Techniques to Connect with Your Teen, Item 3597 $10.95

The Well-Ordered Home, Item 321X $12.95

The Well-Ordered Office, Item 3856 $13.95

10 Simple Solutions to Panic, Item 3252 $11.95

10 Simple Solutions to Shyness, Item 3481 $11.95

The Self-Nourishment Companion, Item 2426 $10.95

The Community Building Companion, Item 2884 $10.95

Serentiy to Go, Item 2353 $12.95

The Daily Relaxer, Item 0695 $12.95

Call **toll free, 1-800-748-6273,** or log on to our online bookstore at **www.newharbinger.com** to order. Have your Visa or Mastercard number ready. Or send a check for the titles you want to New Harbinger Publications, Inc., 5674 Shattuck Ave., Oakland, CA 94609. Include $4.50 for the first book and 75¢ for each additional book, to cover shipping and handling. (California residents please include appropriate sales tax.) Allow two to five weeks for delivery.

Prices subject to change without notice.